FAST REAL ESTATE PROFITS IN ANY MARKET:

The Art of Flipping Properties— Insider Secrets From the Experts Who Do It Every Day

By Sebastian Howell

FAST REAL ESTATE PROFITS IN ANY MARKET: The Art of Flipping Properties—Insider Secrets From the Experts Who Do It Every Day

ISBN-13: 978-0-910627-68-1   ISBN-10: 0-910627-68-9

Library of Congress Cataloging-in-Publication Data

Smith, Amanda C., 1973-
 Fast real estate profits in any market : the art of flipping properties' insider secrets from the experts who do it every day / Amanda C. Smith.
     p. cm.
Includes bibliographical references and index.
 ISBN 0-910627-68-1 (978-0-910627-68-9 : alk. paper)
 1. Real estate investment. 2. House buying 3. House selling. 4. Real estate business. I. Title.

 HD1382.5.S526 2006
 332.63'243--dc22
                    2006012540

EDITOR: Jackie Ness • jackie_ness@charter.net
EDITOR: Ann Brown • Virtual Admins Plus • 800-320-5159 • Info@VirtualAdminsPlus.com www.VirtualAdminsPlus.com
ART DIRECTION & INTERIOR DESIGN: Meg Buchner • megadesn@mchsi.com
FRONT COVER & BOOK PRODUCTION DESIGN: Lisa Peterson, Michael Meister • info@6sense.net
GLOSSARY COMPILED BY: Christina Mohammed

Printed in the United States

TABLE of CONTENTS

CHAPTER 6: FHA/VA LOANS   101

CHAPTER 7: FINDING PROPERTY THAT IS PRIME FOR FLIPPING   107

CHAPTER 8: SELL OR HOLD?   137

CHAPTER 9: RENOVATING PROPERTIES   147

CHAPTER 10: FROM INVESTMENT TO FLIP—THE ART OF SHOWING AND SELLING   189

SUMMARY OF THE PROGRESSION OF A PROPERTY FLIP   205

CONCLUSION   209

REFERENCE   214

INDEX   215

GLOSSARY   219

Alas! Finally someone has written one of the most informative books that should be listed #1 on the required reading list for anyone involved with the acquisition or sale of real estate. I always wondered why I could not find a comprehensive book written about investing in real estate.

After reading *Fast Real Estate Profits in any Market: The Art of Flipping Properties*, I totally understood why it has taken so long. I felt as though the author had been following me around whilst I was working with one of my first customers who needed to do a 1031 within a limited amount of time. Of course he was selling a property in a different state and wanted to acquire one of the properties that I was selling in Mexico. However, after leafing frantically through my RE book and searching the internet I informed him that this would not be considered a 1031. I became his Realtor and he purchased a property that he flipped within a few months. He has flipped four properties since then.

Today almost everyone is interested in real estate. There was a time when property was kept in a family for generations. Those days have almost disappeared in the United States. Even first time homeowners begin the process of flipping before they have made the decision to purchase. As a Realtor I have found that one of the first questions that I am asked is: "Do you think that this property will increase in value and how much did the owner pay for it?" I am constantly being asked questions about investing in real estate by people in various professions.

Because of globalization the world has shrunk. Many of my customers and clients are international and they too are investing and flipping. I am constantly being asked questions about investing in real estate from students to the workers in luxury buildings and garage attendants. Although I am a Certified International Property Specialist who has spent many hours in mandatory real estate classes that were taken in the United States and in Greece, I feel that this book will be a great asset to me as a professional.

EUGENIA C. FOXWORTH
Coldwell Banker Hunt Kennedy
1200 Lexington Ave., New York, NY 10028
212.327.1200, Ext. 263
Fax: 212.327.1231
eugenia.foxworth@cbhk.com
www.eugeniafoxworth.realtor.com
www.cbhk.com

Eugenia Foxworth was elected in 2005 to serve as the President of the New York City Local Council of FIABCI-USA through December 2006. As a Certified Previews Property Specialist, she specializes in exceptional properties in New York City and internationally. She has acquired a reputation with both buyers and sellers as someone who can make a deal happen through her tenacity, knowledge of the market, professionalism and personality. She is licensed with the Real Estate Board of New York and is a member of the Manhattan Association of Realtors, the National Association of Realtors and FIABCI. She is a Coldwell Banker Certified Previews Broker and a Certified International Property Specialist. Eugenia resides in New York and has lived and traveled extensively throughout the world.

i

THE ALLURE OF REAL ESTATE

Are you reading this book because you have concerns about the security of your 401K? Perhaps you are just looking for a way to work on your own terms and still make great money. The initial allure of the real estate world may be different for many people, but the prospects are the same. With potential profits of about 6 percent from sales that are generally in the hundreds of thousands of dollars, property is a hot commodity. Real estate, as a business, perhaps turns out more millionaires per capita than any other. With the odds working for you rather than against you, it is difficult not to be tempted by the potential for financial freedom, the chance to work on your own terms and your own time, and the lifestyle that comes with the independence of being a successful entrepreneur.

Today's corporate business world is unstable. This is no secret. The concerns brought about the constant restructuring and reformation of large American corporations has, for the last decade, played a steady role in the frequent fluctuation of the stock market and is responsible for thousands of displaced workers every year. It is becoming all too clear to many that in 21st century America, real financial security comes from our own perseverance. Having a good job is no longer enough. According to statistics, the average person will have between 7 and 10 jobs during his lifetime. Of those, 3 to 5 will involve major career changes. Those figures support why a growing number of people are now asking themselves what will happen to their family if their corporate jobs are affected by a shift. More and more people are beginning to feel the need to seek the safety net of an alternative source of income, and the advantages of real estate stand on their own merit when measured against other business contingents.

One of the reasons the purchase and sale of property is appealing as a career is because of its ability to quickly rebound from—and even resist—downturns in the economy at large. Think about it. People will always need shelter. It is one of the basic human needs. In addition, the human population is rising at a fairly rapid pace. In fact, the U.S. Census Bureau predicts that the American population will double to almost 600 million people by the year 2100. Housing demands are already mushrooming. Experts predict 14 million new households by 2010. Clearly, the demand for housing is not going to go away and will only continue to rise. More people mean a need for more housing. Real estate may, in fact, be one of the only businesses not susceptible to the increasingly unstable economy and virtually untouchable by constantly changing technology. Even the greatest technological advances are never going to be able to eliminate the need for shelter.

1

WHY REAL ESTATE?

THE UPS AND DOWNS OF REAL ESTATE

The claims of real estate as a lucrative field are genuine, but there are many aspects, both good and bad, to weigh when you consider venturing into the business of real estate. Having the luxury of making your own hours, the opportunity to be your own boss, and potential financial freedom are all trade offs for sporadic opportunity, inconsistent paychecks, and irregular working hours. The following sections are candid looks of the pros and the cons of a career in flipping houses to help you consider all angles while contemplating it as a career.

Although a career as a real estate investor appeals to many people because it can bring large profits quickly, it is not easy money. If you are currently employed full-time, think of everything your current job entails. Now think of the duties of your Manager, Vice President, IT Specialist, and Administrative Assistant. When you become your own employer, you will, at least in the beginning, also be assuming the duties that each of these individuals would perform in their respective roles. You must be prepared to commit yourself full-time to doing whatever it takes to set events in motion and keep them moving forward. Although there is a significant amount of freedom gained when one becomes self employed, the stress bar is raised slightly in the assumption of multiple roles and responsibilities.

It is important to remember that not all of your current financial obligations and responsibilities will disappear simply because you change careers. What this means is that it is essential that you give full consideration to how you will maintain your finances while you get your investing off the ground. This is not only important for lifestyle purposes, but because you are entering into a business in which maintaining an acceptable credit rating is essential.

Health and life insurance are seemingly small details that many people do not consider prior to venturing into business for themselves. If a medium or large sized corporation employs you right now, chances are, they are paying a large portion of your health insurance costs. When you go into business for yourself, you will need to purchase your own health insurance, which can be somewhat pricey. This is an essential added expense that many people erroneously leave off the books when initially evaluating their financial condition.

Make a business plan. Although the early stages of your business will primarily evolve around finding those first properties in which to invest, it is important that you have goals and a plan for achieving them. In a world in which so much is frequently going on, it is very easy to get distracted and lose focus. A solid business plan will help you prioritize and stay on track.

Essentially, there are certain aspects of being in business for yourself that you either can utilize to work for you or, if neglected, can end your dreams of being a successful entrepreneur. Understanding the role of elements and understanding how to use them to your benefit can help you realize your dreams.

TIME

Your time is yours. When you own the business, there are no time clocks or time off requests dictating your work schedule. You decide the demands of your business needs. If you need a morning off to visit the doctor, rather than disrupt your work schedule, it can be built into it. If you want to take a morning exercise class at the gym, that can also be built into your day. You decide what hours and days you work, not someone else. If you prefer to work evenings and/or weekends as opposed to a regular nine to five schedule, this can also be accomplished through entrepreneurship.

The downside to the time aspect of flipping, however, is that your time, to a certain extent, must be coordinated with that of contractors, real estate professionals, and city officials. Visiting the worksite to oversee progress, locating and touring potential investment properties, and obtaining the proper permits and inspections will all be important parts of your business. Completing them will sometimes require you to make compromises in your daily schedule in order to ensure these tasks are accomplished.

You will also sometimes find yourself working odd or irregular hours. For instance, you may be able to ensure you do not work on Thursday mornings so that you can take a real estate class at a local college, but the trade off may be that you find yourself working evening or weekend hours to compensate for it. Likewise, during some phases of a real estate project, you may find that you have scarcely enough work to fill more than a couple of hours of each day. However, as the project picks up pace and nears completion, you may work sixteen, eighteen, or even twenty-hour days to ensure work is completed on time and within budget. In real estate, time is money, and a large part of your success will rest upon how well you are able to budget your time.

In general, though, one of qualities you will notice that increases exponentially during your real estate career will be the way in which you manage time. One day, you will notice that you are exceptionally efficient in the way in which you budget your time. You become so accustomed to making time count in the world of flipping that it becomes almost second nature to make the most of your time. Eventually you will realize that being set free from a cubicle in which you were forced into a daily eight-hour box actually freed your ability to maximize your time.

IT'S YOUR MONEY TO GAIN OR LOSE

You pay yourself. Your hopes for a better income will no longer be limited to whatever raise your company may give you at the end of the fiscal year. Instead, your paycheck will be a direct reflection of your strategy and efforts. Gone will be the days in which your pay increase and salary are interdependent on the efforts of your coworkers. Gone will be the days when your income expectations are limited. Only you will limit your income potential.

Of course, there are certain drawbacks to being wholly financially dependent on your own efforts. Primarily, you must work. If you do not, you will not make any money. Likewise, whereas minor mistakes at your old corporate job may have been absorbed by the sheer size and budget of the company, you will not have the numbers to afford yourself that same luxury. Errors can be costly and even business ending. That means careful consideration must be given to all decisions. Proper management of time, commitments, and budget will literally determine your success or failure. In real estate, it is completely possible to achieve that dream of owning a vacation home in Hawaii. It is also completely possible to find yourself penniless if you are not prepared to commit fully to your efforts.

Of course, in real estate, the old adage that you must have money to make money is somewhat true. Although it is possible to finance or flip property yet incur almost no costs out of pocket, you still must be prepared to meet expenses. You need to allocate properly those funds that you do have and know how to spend in order to get back what you put in, plus a profit. Making the most of every available dollar will be the name of the game in the beginning. As long as you master and do this, you will be successful in the financial aspects of your pursuits.

PEOPLE WILL ALWAYS NEED HOUSING

Whether you are thinking of getting into the flipping business to act as a landlord while property appreciates or you intend to strictly renovate and sell, the need for housing is constant. It is one of the five basic human needs. Population growth and the increase in immigration ensure real estate will always be a steady market that is relatively resistant to economic slumps. A career in real estate means you will not have to worry about your commodity becoming outdated or eliminated by newer and greater inventions. The market is secure. With that security, though, is a certain amount of risk.

Although real estate is steady, income and spending potential are not. Therefore, even though the real estate market often suffers minimal impact in a poor economy, it still takes a hit, nevertheless. It is important to be prepared with a plan for weathering a poor economy. Inevitably, the outlook will rise again and with it, so will the real estate market. However, sometimes you will be forced to either hold a piece of property in order to usurp its full profit potential or sell it at a loss. Chances are, either choice will disrupt your budget and put some sort of temporary financial strain on you. However short-lived the slumps may be, they still hit property owners pretty hard, which makes them an important aspect of the business to consider when thinking of a career as a real estate investor.

RISK IS A PART OF THE BUSINESS

Risk is the one word in real estate that scares most potential investors, but it is something that cannot be eliminated. There will always be risk involved in property flipping. However, with proper research, risk can be assessed and minimized. Risk alone should not keep anyone from a career in real estate, but decisiveness, the ability to analyze a scenario from multiple angles, and comfortableness in situations of chance is essential to managing risk. Those unable to enter into a situation with a certain level of uncertainty should probably give careful consideration to the field of real estate before pursuing a career in flipping houses.

It is important to understand that real estate is not a field into which you can enter half-heartedly and expect to find success. Real estate is a self-paved path, and your heart will determine whether you travel down a good path or a bad one. You will need to own each and every project with an almost passionate zest. Although one of the primary lessons you will reap from this book is that planning is essential, it is equally important to deal with issues of the moment and ensure they are completely resolved before running ahead of yourself. If you do not, you may find yourself with an even bigger mess down the road. If you are the type of person who will assume each property with the attitude that it is nothing but a big headache that you need to unload as soon as possible, then you should probably stop reading and begin reconsidering your career choice, because you will not get very far. As with any career, in order to find success, you need to believe wholeheartedly in what you are doing.

You also have to be willing to stand alone and trust in your own decisions. This sounds very simple to many, but take a moment to really stop and think about the last time you made a choice that was completely uninfluenced by anyone but your own thoughts and conclusions. For most of us, outside influences often play a larger role in our decisions than we are willing to admit. If you do not have a healthy dose of good old-fashioned self-esteem, you will need to build it up before considering real estate any further. You will face many obstacles and rejections that require a person who is confident in the business decisions he or she makes and is certain that his or her goals are attainable.

It is healthy to think as big as you want, but remember that everyone has to start at the beginning. You need to understand that, although you will eventually reach a point of independence with persistence, goals, and a well thought-out plan, as with building any business, it will take some time and work. Do not hurry through the early developing stages. It is important that you understand the reasons for them and take away the lessons you get from them. This is how you gain knowledge and learn the business, which will ultimately make you a better businessperson and make achieving the big dreams possible. The primary mistake that many would-be successful investors make is that everyone wants to be an expert, but few want to invest the time, effort, and energy into becoming one. Just as most scholars did not earn a Ph.D. by merely taking a few classes, you will not become a real estate expert by dabbling.

FULL-TIME VERSUS PART-TIME VENTURES

At first, many potential investors consider a part-time venture into real estate in order to minimize the initial financial impact of the transition. Part-time flipping efforts can work if you intend to purchase property and either live in it or hold it while you refurbish. Living in a property while you renovate will absorb the potential financial burden of an additional mortgage. However, with this option comes the reality of living in a construction site. If you are a person who is accustomed to having everything in your home in a neat, working order, you may want to reconsider a part-time effort in real estate. However, if you love being able to regale your friends with stories of cooking on a Bunsen burner for three weeks while your kitchen was torn apart, then you might find it a pleasurable adventure to live in houses while you are renovating them.

It is still important to remember that even if living in your property while renovating does allow you to maintain your full-time job, in all likelihood, you will still find yourself taking time off to take care of business at the house. Inspectors, in particular, tend to do their rounds during normal business hours. If you fail to meet with an inspector, your construction will literally be halted until you do. In addition, even if your renovations go smoothly, you will still find yourself preoccupied with what is happening with the project, which may inhibit your ability to focus elsewhere and ultimately affect the quality of your work at your full-time job. Therefore, it is a good idea to take a candid look at how intense your full-time job is before conclusively deciding to flip part-time.

If you find yourself frequently bringing your work home with you or are often thinking about work matters after you have left the office, it is probably a good idea to decide if maintaining your full-time job or pursuing a career in real estate is more important to you now. Inevitably, if you attempt to split yourself part-time between two full-time efforts, you will fail at one of the two. Not only are you not being honest with yourself, you are being unfair to the contractors handling the project you have undertaken as a flip, as well as to your boss and coworkers at your full-time job, since both expect and require a full-time effort.

Proper consideration should also be given to the quality of your family life, if you are considering adding a part-time effort to your full-time job. If you cannot remember the last time you attended one of your child's soccer games because you have been so preoccupied with your full-time job, it probably is not a good idea to add a part-time job that will only interfere even further into family matters. On the other hand, if your full-time job requires such dedication from you that you feel your child's life is passing you by without your having the luxury of enjoying it, it might be time to consider exchanging such a demanding full-time job for a career. Real estate allows you the flexibility and opportunity to make improvements to the quality of your family life.

A particular part-time opportunity that can be used to generate cash for those who simply do not have the option of leaving their full-time jobs until they are able to build up some sort of savings to live off for a period of time is to purchase a rental property that turns enough cash to meet their mortgage plus a small profit. You should be prepared, however, for the responsibilities that come with being a landlord. You will be expected to maintain the property, which will also take time, albeit not the same amount of time required to oversee a large renovation project. Another drawback to this approach is that it is definitely not the speediest route between point A and point B. Often times, after maintenance costs are deducted, the income from a single rental property is not significant enough to reinvest right away. It often takes years of appreciation before rental properties really begin to pay investors back, which may be more time than what many are willing to wait.

Sometimes a partner can provide the balance needed to make a part-time pursuit a viable option. Since the responsibilities will be split between the two of you, a large portion of the burden you would otherwise carry yourself is alleviated. You can take turns visiting the site, speaking with contractors, and meeting with inspectors. Of course, with a partnership, you must be certain that both parties are completely aware of individual expectations and are in agreement with them. If not, what you will end up with may be a full-time mess rather than a part-time job. In addition, with a partner, your profits will be split in half as well. The upside, though, is that two people usually begin with twice the pull when it comes to financing, unless one of you enters into the partnership as an investor.

The moral here is that, in general, whether you ultimately decide to keep your day job or not, flipping is still a full-time effort. So, it doesn't so much come down to a decision of whether to pursue real estate full-time or part-time as it does a decision about whether you realistically have the capabilities — mental and physical — to juggle two full-time careers while maintaining a healthy lifestyle.

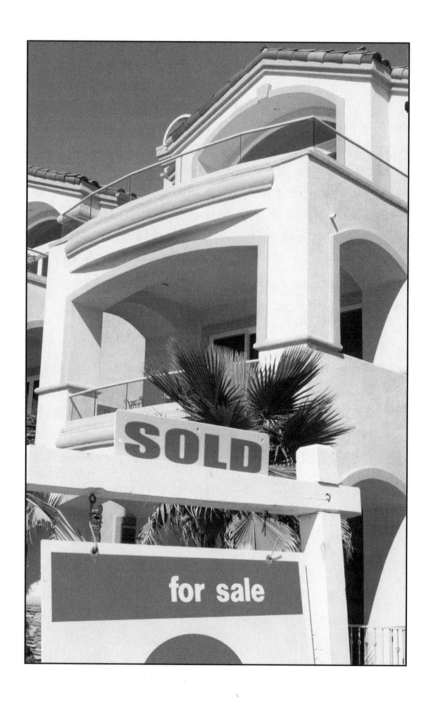

2

WHAT IS FLIPPING?

F lipping houses is the term coined to describe buying properties, investing minimum time and money in renovations, and then reselling for a profit. In the process, a house goes from being an outdated fixer-upper to a model property within its respective neighborhood. Thus, the investor "flips" the house. There are two techniques of flipping and two types of investors. Some will argue that there are actually three types of flippers, but for the purposes of this book, we will place the third one in a different category to be discussed in a later chapter. Since the method of flipping specifically corresponds to a type of flipper, we will discuss them simultaneously.

DEALERS

Dealers are individuals who, more or less, act as middlemen in a real estate transaction. In doing so, they never actually take possession of the property. A dealer locates properties that are on the market for a price well below their market values, usually because they are in need of some work or repair. Once the dealer finds a property that he or she thinks has potential, it will be assessed of its value to determine if it could be bought and immediately resold at a higher price. If the dealer decides there is enough potential in the property to earn a profit in the immediate resale and yet still hold, within its walls, the opportunity for a second party to earn a profit after repairs and refurbishing, he or she will then shop around for an interested investor, usually one who is known to be in the market of renovating properties, before buying the property. After finding a willing buyer, the dealer will offer to sell the property to the investor at a higher price than that which he will be paying, but is still significantly below the property's market value. The dealer will then work with his agent and the property owner, negotiate the purchase of the property, and, at the actual closing, the dealer will buy the property for the price which he negotiated and then immediately sell the property to his investor at the price they negotiated. The profit, for the dealer, is the difference between the price at which he bought the property and the price at which he resold it, and his role with this property is complete. The dealer is now free to move on to the next one. Thus, the primary function of a dealer is to create a three-way, win-win-win situation for the real estate agent, himself, and the investor. The real estate agent not only gets commission, but often unloads a troublesome or otherwise hard to sell property in the process. The dealer makes a slight profit for himself in the immediate flip of the property, and the investor, who is often the next type of flipper we will discuss, purchases a property at a rate that will allow him to renovate it and put it back on the market for a price that will potentially earn him a much higher profit than that earned by either the real estate agent or the dealer. Thus, in the world of real estate, the term dealer is somewhat synonymous with wholesaler.

Although the role of the dealer is appealing to many because it is very brief, requires very little — and sometimes no — out of pocket money, and does not require any extended knowledge of construction or repair, there are drawbacks to being a dealer. First and foremost, the profits earned by dealers are significantly lower than those of retailers, which are the next type of flippers we will discuss and usually the type of investors to whom dealers market properties. However, upon examination, it is easy to see why per property earnings are significantly less for dealers than retailers.

A dealer has only minimum investment of time and money in a piece of property, and his profit reflects this. A retailer, however, will put considerably more time and money into a property purchased from a dealer in order to restore it to retail market condition. Since retail profits are significantly higher than wholesale ones, the retailer makes more money per property. However, since the dealer's involvement with flipping usually ends at the closing, a dealer can flip many more houses in a year than a retailer. Thus, the true money for a dealer is often not in the profit earned from individual transactions but in the number of properties flipped in a year.

Another problem for dealers is technicalities. This is why many dealers either are or once were real estate agents. There are many stipulations to how a house may be transferred legally without a buyer assuming possession. Only certain types of mortgages and titles can be used for immediate transfer. This means that lenders, types of loans, and even the type of sale that is done on a property must be carefully orchestrated in order for the transaction to remain both ethical and legal. Therefore, although being a dealer does not require many "fix-it" skills, it is necessary for dealers to do their homework and keep abreast of real estate law. For those who are starting from the very beginning and have never dealt in real estate, a few real estate courses at a local college also may be in order.

RETAILERS

The second type of flipper is the one with which most people associate the concept of flipping. Retailers are individuals who purchase properties at a price significantly below their market values, because they are in need of repair. They fix them up and then put them back on the market at a much higher price. When the house sells, the difference of the original price the retailer paid for the property and the cost of refurbishing, subtracted from the selling price, becomes the profit. Although these types of real estate flippers net much higher profits than dealers, there is also a significantly higher risk involved in retail flipping. Retailers actually take possession of the property and spend large amounts of money to make necessary repairs and improvements needed to restore the house to retail condition. There is a lot more time and money involved in this scenario and, therefore, a lot more to lose. If a project goes over time or budget or fails to sell at the price a retailer originally anticipated, it can be very costly. Therefore, to be a successful retail flipper requires significant skills in organization and time management.

When analyzing a prospective property, a retailer must determine the amount of work that needs to be done to the property, the amount of time it will take, the growth potential for the neighborhood in which the property is located, and the low, average, and high selling prices of other homes in the area. The retailer then must decide the budget needed to restore the property to a condition that will reap a price within the comparative expectations of the neighborhood, yet still generate a profit. Although this sounds very simple, it often involves some very careful and detailed formulaic figures, which we will examine more closely in a later chapter.

Of course, as we have examined, the primary drawback to flipping houses as a retailer is the commitment of time and money. Because renovating houses requires both, a retailer often flips significantly less properties per year than a dealer, but often at a much higher profit. With more potential earnings to gain, however, there is more to lose. If a project runs significantly over time or budget, does not sell for its anticipated price, or a market slump hits in the middle of renovations, the result could be financially devastating. When a project is finished on time and within budget, however, and sells quickly, the profits are often significant. Because of this, it is possible for a retailer to live off the profits of a few good flips each year. Sometimes, in retail flipping, success is found in quality and not quantity. Finding your retail niche, however, is something that, to an extent, can only come from experience and practice. Many retailers have refined their method and style of flipping over time to be almost unique to them.

BEING THE BEST

You will rarely read about people who make partial or insincere efforts while trying to become the best in their chosen field. That is because you must put your heart into your pursuits and believe in what you are doing. Before even evaluating your qualities and potentials, you must first ask yourself how strong your passion for real estate is. If it is merely lukewarm, perhaps you should continue looking. However, if you are so intent and determined about your pursuits that you have already laid out your plans on paper and are hungry to get started, then you have a very strong chance of being successful, as long as you can match your talents to your ambitions.

However, being a businessperson requires a strong constitution that is made up of many demanding qualities. Without these characteristics, it will be very difficult to achieve your goals and conduct business. If you see that you fall short of any of them, consider working to improve the particular qualities in which you feel you are lacking, or, if possible, further your education in order to improve them.

While reading the description of each type of flipping and the two different types of flippers, some necessary skills for success may be obvious. Nevertheless, many others are essential and often not considered or are overlooked when an individual is considering a career in flipping houses. The following are a few objectives that you will want to evaluate candidly in relation to you.

ORGANIZATION

Whether you are considering a career as a Dealer or a retailer, you must be organized. From small things, such as knowing what questions to ask when scoping out a property, i.e., knowing who you called, when you talked to them, and where you filed your notes and numbers, to large chores, such as making sure the correct paperwork and permits are filed, you must know how to create structure and coherency in your partnerships, in your paperwork, and in building your team.

Real estate is all about planning. Operating blindly in the world of investing is business suicide. A lot of your success will be determined by how well you are able to plan and organize.

DISCIPLINE

The initial appeal of being your own boss can quickly give way to despair if you cannot exercise discipline. Although you will often be working on your own schedule, you will still need to work. You will find yourself facing many deadlines, and your success as a real estate flipper will greatly depend on your ability to follow through with the work that needs to be done to meet them. Discipline is also essential in keeping your project on time and on budget. Remember; you are the boss. That means that you will be the one responsible for keeping construction on schedule, for appropriately scheduling contractors, and for making decisions about the budget. All of this requires discipline.

PROJECT MANAGEMENT

For dealers, this specifically relates to knowing when the timing is right to jump on a project and to ensure everything and everyone are lined up correctly in order for the flip to happen. For retailers, project management is much more extensive and critical to a project. If you are a retailer who has just purchased a property, you are now faced with the responsibility of determining whether the work to be done can be DIY (Do It Yourself) or professional in nature. Then, you must determine the budget for the project. If you decide that you will need to hire contractors to complete all or some of the work, you will need to review not only the costs of their proposals in relation to your budget, but also the timeline in which they can complete the work. Once you hire contractors whose bids align with your timeline and budget, you are then responsible for scheduling the work so that it coordinates with the jobs being done. For example, it would not really make much sense to schedule a cabinet installer to come install the cabinets that have not yet been delivered. You will also be responsible for ensuring that work and costs stay on par to your plan. You will need to reevaluate and adjust your plan for unanticipated costs and delays in a way that will prevent them from significantly shrinking or even completely eliminating your profit. You will need to know when it is time to talk to contractors, ensure all permits are in order, and confirm the work being done is in accordance with local codes.

DETAIL ORIENTED

When evaluating a property's potential, you must be able to see all of the things that make it either a good or bad investment, because it is those little things that will eventually either add up to big profit or a big loss. Likewise, you must understand the details in the contracts you negotiate. You must consider all of those little clauses that may be overlooked and can cost you dearly or give you an edge that others in the same field do not enjoy.

GOOD NEGOTIATION SKILLS

Real estate, as with many businesses, is all about the bottom line. Being able to manipulate numbers to fit into the amounts you have figured is essential from the beginning to the end of the flipping process. You must negotiate the purchase price of a property so that you will still have room to earn a profit in its resale, you must be able to negotiate both time and labor rates with contractors, and you must be able to negotiate the final selling price of the property. If you cannot or will not negotiate, real estate is not the career path for you.

Negotiations are discussed in depth later in this book. Remember that negotiation is not a peacemaking effort, but a deal-making one. Enough cannot be said about how important it is for you to hone your ability to take control and work a good deal. This not only requires you to be fair, but also shrewd. You have to be willing to take the risks that are sometimes involved in edgy negotiations. Realizing the payoff of your negotiation efforts is as important as working the deal itself.

GOOD COMMUNICATION SKILLS

You must be able to establish clearly your needs and expectations in all facets of the business. This is not exclusive to verbal communication. You must be able to conduct a professional telephone call, write an effective e-mail, and compose comprehensible business documents. Without these abilities, you will have a lot of difficulty in the flipping business. It is also important to remember that communication involves listening too. It is critical to be able to hear, comprehend, and respond to what is communicated to you, not just what you communicate to others. Doing so in a manner that exudes integrity, sense, and consideration will determine not only the success of an individual project, but also your success as an entrepreneur. If you build a reputation as someone who is difficult to communicate with, eventually other professionals in the business will not want to work with you, and you will begin to find it increasingly difficult to get the work you need completed at the price you need to have it done.

FLEXIBILITY

You are going to get many punches thrown at you in real estate, and you are going to have to learn to roll with them. Deals fall through, players change, contractors overbook and underestimate, inspectors miss flaws in need of repair, weather is less than cooperative, and the list goes on. In short, you will find that very few projects will actually happen from beginning to end and exactly as you plan them. Learning to recover and regroup when they do not is not only crucial; it is part of the fun of flipping.

MOTIVATION AND STAMINA

I group these two together, because one is more or less the continuation of the other. Motivation is the force it takes to get a project rolling, and stamina is the inertia it takes to keep it moving. In the beginning, you must be motivated to make money, you must be motivated to make a piece of property better, and you must be motivated to see that the project realizes completion. While the project is underway, you must have the stamina to maintain your efforts through to the end. If you become bored quickly, have trouble focusing, or are easily distracted, then you may want to think about how to improve your motivation and stamina before entering into a career as a real estate flipper. Stamina is also crucial to those who plan to do a lot of their own construction and improvement projects. Professionals who have been doing it for years can make it look easy, but installing a hardwood floor, for instance, can take a lot out of you, which is important to your timeline. If you figure lying the hardwood floor of a living room will take only a day, but you become too tired halfway through the day to continue or are too exhausted the next day to complete the project for that day, your project timeline has been disrupted. Even though one day may not appear to make a big impact, several days of similar events will eventually add up. In a business in which time literally is money, having the stamina to stay on target is critical to success.

As you can see, beginning a career in real estate involves some decisions that involve taking an honest look at one's own skill set. In a sense, you must interview yourself to determine how successful you will be in the real estate business. Above all, you must be straightforward when doing this. If you are not, you will ultimately end up broke and frustrated instead of affluent and successful. If you find weaknesses in those areas crucial to success, determine how you can improve them. The good news is that just about every skill required for the successful real estate entrepreneur is one that can be learned. Because you find that you are not particularly strong in a specific skill now does not mean that, with a bit of focus, practice, and maybe even education or training, you cannot improve your abilities in that area. Being able to make good decisions is a big factor in the success of any entrepreneur, and this includes the beginning steps, those you take before you even begin searching for your first property.

3

THE PLAYERS

There are almost as many players in the real estate game as there are properties. Understanding how each of them fits into the grand scheme and the role each plays is essential. It is important for you as an investor to be able to utilize all of your resources to their fullest potential. You will need to know how to balance managing these people at times while humbly heeding to their advice during others. Maintaining control of your situation at all times is the key. This is your business and your money. You will need to act in the best interest of that business. At the same time, many of the individuals you will be working with will also be working in the interests of their business and money. Learning to tell the difference and leveraging the two will be the secret to unlocking your success.

LAWYERS

Although attorneys are often intimidating, they are an essential part of real estate. Real estate law is complicated and bureaucratic, and it changes often. Having a professional on your payroll who is up on those changes and who can effectively keep you aware of them is invaluable. When large amounts of contract work are involved, an attorney can advise you about some of the legal aspects of contracting that you may easily overlook. Your attorney can also help you compose the necessary paperwork for buying or selling a property and make sure the right type of property exchange takes place. Therefore, finding a real estate lawyer who is knowledgeable and who can make you feel comfortable is perhaps one of the most critical moves you will make in the business. You will depend on your lawyer to review and compose contracts with your best interests in mind. Your lawyer is not only your legal eyes, but your ethical ones as well. Therefore, it is important to find an attorney who is sort of a reflection of yourself.

Start by finding lawyers in your area who specialize in real estate. An attorney who specializes in real estate will be the most educated and knowledgeable in the field. Once you locate several lawyers in your area, meet and interview them. If you can, do this in person or, if you find one or two in particular that you really like after conducting initial phone interviews, schedule a consultation with them, so that you can introduce yourself, explain your business plan, and determine if there is chemistry for a working relationship. It is crucial that you feel comfortable with your attorney. Even if you find one who seems particularly educated in the field, if you do not feel comfortable with him or her, keep looking.

Once you find a lawyer with whom you are comfortable, it is important to determine not only his rate structure, but also exactly what those rates entail. The trust in even the best working relationships can be shattered when unexpected surprises turn up on invoices. Make sure you clarify whether you are being a charged a flat or hourly rate for services. If you are being charged hourly, confirm exactly when service commences and ends. When you contact your attorney to perform a duty that he does not regularly do for you, ask him how much you will be charged or to explain how he will be billing you for the service.

Be honest with your lawyer. He can be a great tool in your success, but he must know and understand your position before he can truly do so to the best of his ability. If you have concerns about a property or project, share them with your attorney. He will be able to help you determine the best next steps, which may not always be something that you are ready for or are willing to accept right away. Your lawyer is objective. He is the one who will take the emotional aspects of the business out of the picture and advise you solely on facts.

When selecting an attorney, be careful to avoid conflicts of interest, which can exist in many forms. Real estate lawyers are often, themselves, also investors. Likewise, they may represent other investors or even local real estate brokers or agencies. It is important to locate a lawyer who is acting in the best interest of his clients, not his own agenda. You do not need to find a lawyer who does not represent others in the same field. In fact, you would probably find that task a virtual impossibility. However, you should feel confident that the attorney you select can act in the best interests of his clients independently and not according to his own agenda or the agenda of a particularly high paying client. A professional attorney should and will advise you that there are potential conflicts of interest during your consultation and provide you with any applicable information that will help you make a decision without violating the privacy of his clients. If a lawyer does express such a concern to you, give serious consideration to what he tells you. The conflict may be something that can be resolved or overcome. On the other hand, it may be best to find another attorney.

BROKERS AND AGENTS

First, we should start out by distinguishing the difference between a broker and an agent. The only real difference is that, in most states, only a broker is actually licensed to list property, whereas an agent sells property. Both titles require some form of education and training as well as a license to either list or sell property in the state in which they do business. Typically, most buyers work with an agent while most sellers work with both a broker and an agent.

To further complicate matters, in the contemporary world of real estate, you will often find yourself working with both sellers' and buyers' agents. A sellers' agent is the traditional real estate professional that many associate with the purchase or sale of a home. He is simply someone homeowners contract to sell their home in exchange for a commission from the sell.

A buyers' agent is a more recent addition to commonplace real estate transactions and is a professional hired by individuals interested in purchasing a house. Some buyers simply do not have the time or the desire to search for property themselves, so they hire an objective professional to do it for them. This can be both a good and a bad thing for sellers. On one hand, a buyers' agent is impartial. Unlike with typical homebuyers, who can form an attachment to a piece of property based on emotion, sentiment seldom plays a role in the decisions of a buyers' agent. Instead, the buyers' agent has been given provided with a list of needs and wants of the buyer he or she represents and evaluates homes based solely on those guidelines. However, this can sometimes work against a seller. Sometimes, when a home appeals to the emotions of buyers, that aspect can be used as a selling tool. For instance, even though the entire house needs new carpet, if the kitchen reminds a potential buyer of her grandmother's kitchen and evokes good memories from her childhood, she might be persuaded to buy the house, in spite of the expense and headache of having to install new carpet. A buyers' agent, however, is simply going to make a note that the house needs new carpet. If the buyer has stipulated that the house must have new carpet or carpet that is in good condition, the house will be crossed off the list without any consideration to any sentimental appeal any other part of it might have had.

So, what is the advantage of using a buyers' agent and how do they earn their money? For a particularly busy buyer, using a buyers' agent simplifies the search process and significantly shortens it by quickly weeding out those properties that do not fit what the buyer is looking for. Buyers' agents earn their commission in several ways. Sometimes, a seller's agent will offer to divide his commission with a buyer's agent who can produce a viable purchaser. In other situations, it is actually the buyer who is paying the agent's fee, but be forewarned that some buyers will slip clauses into their offers stipulating that the seller will pay the commission for the buyer's agent.

Because those who flip houses can often find themselves paying the commissions for the both the buyer's and the seller's agents in a single transaction, many who look to get into flipping attempt to avoid the use of professionals all together. Although this may initially net higher profits, it can be detrimental. As the sources with the most inside information about local properties, real estate professionals are your lifeline in the world of flipping. Good ones cannot only tell you what properties are on the market, they can also tell you what properties will be coming on the market. They can also tell you what neighborhoods are booming and which ones are dying. All of these are reasons why it is important to find a local real estate agent with a reputation for being dynamic in the field in the area you intend to target. Then, talk with this person. Let him or her know who you are and that you are looking to begin a career flipping houses. Chances are, he or she will be happy to give you the lowdown on local properties and maybe even give you a briefing on your competition. In the end, the commission fees of a real estate professional often pay for themselves in the form of the invaluable resourcefulness of the agent.

Finding a regular agent with whom you can form a sort of partnership can be one of the best moves you make for your business. If you work regularly with a particular agent, over time, that agent will come to know exactly what you are looking for and may even begin to tip you off about potential properties before they hit the market. To that agent, it is a guaranteed commission. This also alleviates you of much of the time-consuming burden of finding properties, because you will have someone already looking for you. Spending less time locating your next flip allows you to dedicate more time to your current one, which translates to a faster turnaround and a larger profit.

The areas of specialization in real estate are varied. For the most part, real estate investors work with residential brokers or agents who specialize in investment properties. In some regions, mostly in and around larger cities, a distinction is drawn between those professionals who deal strictly with retail residential and those who specialize in investment properties. However, in the majority of cities and towns, investment and retail property is handled by the same firm. In these cases, certain agents will often specialize in investment properties. If this is the case in your area, when you begin searching for an agent, be sure to tell those professionals whom you interview that you have a particular interest in investment property.

The truth is, finding the right real estate professional can be a bit like dating. You may have relationships of varying lengths and intimacies with several people before you find the one that you want to stick with for life. In summation, some tips to keep in mind during your search include:

- **Find a visionary.** When it comes to investment property, it is important to work with someone who can see beyond cosmetics. An agent who seems to recognize or comment on such aspects as the foundation, bone structure, character, woodworking, layout, etc., as opposed to one who focuses on aspects such as paint color, wallpaper, or carpeting is usually a bit more on the visionary side.

- **Make sure there is no conflict of interest.** The simple truth is that many real estate professionals are investors themselves. If you are only ever going to be getting hand me downs that your broker or agent has passed up, then there could be a conflict of interest. This does not mean that having an agent who is also an investor is bad. However, if you find yourself in that particular situation, it is a good idea to make sure that either the type of properties in which you invest or your target area is different from that of your realtor. This will allow you to form a healthy camaraderie without threatening your relationship or your business with unhealthy competition.

- **Conversation is important.** You will be doing a lot of talking to your agent. You should feel comfortable talking candidly to your agent and feel confident in the advice he or she gives you. It is difficult, though, to address the conversational aspects of your relationship with your agent without also discussing tact. Although you may become very close with your realtor, it is very important that business can also become professional and that your agent equally recognize when a decision should be primarily deferred to you.

- **The agent should know your target area.** This is not strictly a reference to geography. A good professional will also know if there are any government grants or tax breaks available for property improvements in the area. A particularly adept professional will also be able to offer you some useful information such as the crime rate and whether or not it is rising or declining.

- **You should never feel pressured to purchase a property.** The trick to being a good agent is not so much knowing how to sell a house, but to whom. In short, if your agent is a good listener, he or she will be able to recognize when a piece of property may not be a good fit for you, and will not attempt to box you into a purchase you really do not want to make.

- **Find a realtor who can close the deal.** Your realtor should know what motivates both buyers and sellers. A sale is a two-way street, so your professional should know how to read the needs of sellers as well as of buyers.

ACCOUNTANTS

Accountants are individuals who cannot only keep your money straight, but can help you take maximum advantage of governmental tax breaks. Since your accountant will be handling the money matters of your business, it goes without saying that your accountant should be someone with whom you are comfortable discussing the details of your finances. If you can, find an accountant who is also knowledgeable about real estate. These individuals will be the most current about the various tax breaks provided to those individuals who purchase investment property. We will discuss these laws in more detail in a later chapter. As in your search for a lawyer and a real estate professional, interview several accountants who have a reputation in the field and who are known to specialize in real estate, and find one with whom you click.

It is understood that being honest with your accountant is critical. Not only is it important for him to know where you stand financially, but the clearer the picture you can paint him of what is really going on the better he can advise you, not merely how to spend your money, but how to earn it and where to go to get the capital you need. Hiding big mistakes or dark spots from your financial past will hurt you and will prevent your accountant from being able to do his job accurately. He has to know what is going on and before he can make an honest and fair assessment.

Once you find an accountant with whom you work well and whom you trust, consider utilizing his talents to manage your various project budgets. He can be a great source in helping you move on from projects that can eventually become money pits. If he is controlling the reins, it is easier for him to stay firm about the stopping point in your budget than it will be for you, because your accountant is concerned only with your bottom line and has not formed the sentimental attachment to a property that you have. When you have poured sweat, tears, and lots of your own money into something, it is easy to become personally attached to a project. Your accountant, however, is concerned about your financial well-being. His attachment is to your finances, and when he starts to see them becoming unhealthy, he will draw the line at a point where you might not be able.

When seeking out an accountant for a real estate business, it is a good idea to find one who specializes in real estate. Many intricate tax laws come into play in the world of real estate, and you are going to need someone who is familiar with them and how to apply them. An accountant whose primary clientele has been manufacturing businesses, for example, may be very good in a manufacturing setting, but if he is not familiar with real estate, then his expertise may not seem so strong in handling your affairs. If an accountant tells you he is familiar with real estate laws, ask him what other clients he has that in the property investment business. If a potential accountant claims to have real estate knowledge but has no clients in that business, it is probably a good idea to keep searching.

Time is money in real estate, so it is also important to find an accountant who is responsive. When you interview accountants, tell them you expect this. If they cannot deliver, keep looking. If you hire an accountant who says he can give your affairs priority on a moment's notice and then does not, find a new accountant. Real estate is a fast-paced environment. The difference of a few hours can cost you a property and, subsequently, potentially a rather large profit. An accountant who costs you more money than he helps you save or earn is not an asset to your business.

LENDERS

There are about as many different types of lenders as there are loans they provide. The various types of loans as well as their pros and cons will be examined in a later chapter. However, securing the right type of lender can be critical, particularly for those with less than perfect credit. Large, nationally based lenders often use a standardized process for making decisions. Often times, the department making the decision is headquarter-based, and depending on whether the company's headquarters happen to be in the city in which you are attempting to purchase property, most of those making the decisions know nothing about you or the property you are trying to assume, other than the numbers that are in front of them. They are, therefore, going to make their decision based on the risk calculated by their computer. If the formulas of the computer software they use calculate a risk for you and the property that is good, then a national lender can be a good choice. There tends to be more stability in national institutions as well. If a sense of security is important to you, you may want to seek a mortgage through a nationally based institution. However, if you are looking for a more personable relationship with your potential lender, then seek out loans through smaller, local institutions.

Smaller institutions are often more flexible in their decision-making capabilities and are more familiar with the local neighborhoods. Although a more localized institution is still going to calculate and consider the risks of granting a loan to you, they are more likely to be in a position to consider you as an individual. In short, it is often possible to plead your case and have other factors fairly considered before a decision is made exclusively based on numbers. Smaller, local lenders may also be in a position to know that the property that does not appear to be such a good risk on paper, may actually be in an area that is experiencing a rebirth or is about to boom in popularity, which may just be enough to persuade them to grant the loan.

Some companies are in the business of exclusively financing home loans. These companies often have many different styles of loans to meet the needs of very a diversified pool of clients. Because of this, they are often more willing to work with those who have had credit issues in the past or are still working to rehabilitate their credit. These types of businesses have been the saving grace for many would-be homeowners who were unable to secure financing through a traditional banking institution. The drawback to these types of institutions, however, is that because they are in the business of mortgages, they are very familiar with the various ways that investors like to bend and play with them. Because of this, mortgage companies often attach clauses to their loans that prevent them from becoming the victims of a bad investment trade off. Therefore, would-be flippers might find themselves wading through more red tape in buying and selling with financing from these companies than with traditional banks.

Be wary of newly formed lending agencies or companies. Ideally, a potential lender will have been in business for several years. If a new lender is a branch or subsidiary of a larger, well-known company, than it is probably safe to do business there, even if it is a new establishment. Nevertheless, if you do not recognize the name or a new lender is not affiliated with a larger organization, proceed with caution. In the past, national headlines and news stories have spread the tragic tales of unknowing investors who lost their life's savings to a mortgage lending company that simply vanished one day or shut its doors with virtually no notice and no way for customers to recoup their money. Make sure a potential lender is licensed and that there are no complaints on file with the Better Business Bureau. If there are, review the files carefully to consider whether or not the issues were resolved satisfactorily.

Make sure potential lenders know their products and services. This may seem like simple common sense, but it is a large enough trap that it still manages to snare many unsuspecting consumers. For some lenders, the issue may simply be a matter of better educating their employees, or their motives may actually be questionable. However, some lenders appear to use a tactic similar to the old-fashioned bait and switch, in which they lure buyers in with one loan offer and then either talk them into a different loan or trap them into one by disqualifying them for the first. Just remember that old-fashioned rule of thumb that if something appears too good to be true, it probably is. If a lender tempts you with a great loan and irresistible interest rate, make sure you read the fine print before signing, and always have a backup plan.

When you approach a lender about a deal, it is important that they understand you are purchasing the property for investment purposes. Some loans do not work well — or at all — with flipping houses, and it is important for the lender to understand that you will not be holding on to the property for long, so that they may: 1) ensure they offer a loan program to fit you, and 2) offer the right type of loan to you. It is also important for you to do your homework and be aware of the lenders' products and services, in order to protect your own interest and which ones might be best for you. Many lenders invoke penalties on the early payoff of traditional loans. Since lenders are in the business of making money as well, it is a good idea to have at least some idea of what your needs are in order to prevent yourself from being locked into a loan that is ultimately going to cost you money. Relying on your lender to tell you is not typically a good idea, since lenders are businesses and not philanthropists.

If you can, find a lender that has some sort of special program for investment properties. Most investment property is so categorized because it is in need of some level of repair upon purchase. Lenders like to feel assured that they are extending a loan on a property that can support those numbers. Your credit may be excellent, but that alone is not going to be enough if the property is not substantial enough to support the mortgage. You may encounter more obstacles or difficulty convincing a lender who does not have any sort of special interest in investment properties to take a gamble on a property that you have intentions to flip.

BUYERS AND SELLERS

Of course, those with whom you may very well have the most contact with as a flipper are other buyers and sellers. There are two types of each — those who are in the business of real estate and those who are not. Retail buyers are the everyday, average Joe home seekers. They are looking for a house in which they intend to live. Although they may sometimes be willing to do minimal rehab or repair in exchange for a lower buying price, they are often looking for a home that is in move-in condition and are not willing to purchase a piece of property that is in need of extensive work. You will most likely market your renovated properties as a retail flipper to these buyers. These customers do not view a property for its potential profitability. They are evaluating it based on its potential to be a comfortable home that meets the needs of their family and is a good buy for its asking price and location. Selling points for these customers will be matters of convenience, such as the proximity to local shopping and recreation; the quality of the local school system; and the general camaraderie amongst the neighbors.

Investment buyers, on the other hand, will be competing with you to purchase properties for the prospective earnings they can produce. Dealers most often work with these buyers. They evaluate properties based solely on their potential, not as they stand in the current situation. An investment buyer can envision a house that may appear to be a wreck to a retail buyer as a refinished masterpiece. These are the buyers you want to target if you are hoping to sell a piece of property that retail buyers may not have the time, patience, or money in which to invest. However, investment buyers are going to be looking for a low, often times near wholesale, price for the property in return for assuming it in its current condition in need of repair.

In the world of selling, a retail flipper is, of course, looking for a retail buyer. This is the person who is willing to pay retail for a nice home. Other investors will not be interested in your property unless they feel they can make some improvement to it that will net them a profit over what they paid. One exception to this may be the marketing of multi-unit or rental properties. Some investors focus on rental properties. They purchase these types of properties, rent them out as landlords, and use the payments from their tenants to pay the mortgage while the property appreciates in value, and then they resell several years later for a profit.

The trick for investment buyers is to find a motivated seller with a property in need of just enough repairs that will cause retail buyers to hesitate, but is still minimal enough that renovations can be completed in a reasonable amount of time, usually within four to six weeks. A motivated seller can be many things. He can be someone who has recently been transferred by his employer and needs to sell quickly, someone who has made an offer on another property that is contingent on the sale of their current one, someone who is seeking to avoid or resolve financial difficulties, or someone who is in the process of a divorce or on the verge of foreclosure and is being forced to sell. Once a motivated seller is located, negotiating a price that leaves plenty of room for a good profit in the end is typically very realistic.

Retail sellers, however, are those individuals who are looking to make a good profit from the sale of their home and are willing to wait for the right offer to come along. They are in no hurry to sell their property if the price is not right. This type of seller is often what the retail flipper becomes upon completion of a project, since the goal has been to bring the house to a condition that places it within the average home price range in the neighborhood in which it is located.

Whether you are the buyer or seller, consider the advantages from the perspective of the other party in relation to the property. What might be motivating him? Is there something he is not telling you that could give you an advantage? If you have ever seen the movie *The Money Pit*, then you do not need this book to know that there is usually a reason when the price of a house sounds too good to be true. Remember, just because a property needs improvement does not make it a good investment. If you are on the buying end, bring a home inspector with you to identify problems that the seller may not be telling you, or that he may not even know about. There is a very good chance that a motivated seller is not attempting to con you at all; he is simply unaware of some of the problems with the house. If you are on the selling end, be conservative with your asking price until you know how serious a potential buyer is. He may just be fishing to see how easily you will waiver so that he can gauge how much room he has to work with. If you have a specific number in mind, do not begin lowering it until you are both absolutely certain you cannot realistically expect to get that number, and that the buyer who is attempting to wheel and deal with you is seriously contemplating making an offer and not just looking for an opening to sucker you.

CONTRACTORS

If you become a retail flipper, you will interact with contractors. Finding reputable contractors who can complete your job at a price within your budget is essential to your success in the business. Locating a contractor who can do the work and has the time to commit to your project can be somewhat disheartening and somewhat of a catch-22. Many reputable contractors are so busy that they are simply unable to commit to completing a project within your timeline. They should be honest with you about this and, when they are, it is wise to re-evaluate how important it is to you to have that particular contractor do your work. If the project can be completed by someone else, keep looking. Finding a good contractor and reusing him for all or most of your work can be a good move for you in the end. Eventually, the contractor may cut you deals or discount his regular rates in exchange for the regular work.

Contractors can be somewhat of a mystery figure for many who have never hired or dealt with one before. Use the rule of three. The rule of three is a common contracting rule in which you commit to reviewing at least three bid proposals prior to hiring a contractor. Merely flipping open your yellow pages to a random listing and calling the first number that catches your attention will not generally yield the best results. If you know anyone who has had the type of work that you need done recently, ask him who he used and if he would recommend that contractor. Many contractors will ask their clients if they can display signs disclosing that their business is doing the work on the house. Drive your target neighborhood and look for these signs. Copy the information from those signs where you find the work impressive.

Once you have gathered at least three names and numbers, call those contractors and interview them. Be sure you are fully prepared to disclose the details of the work you need, your budget, and your timeline. Anyone who is truly professional should and will immediately advise you if he cannot submit a bid that is within your budget and time frame. If this happens, ask the contractor if he can recommend anyone who could perform the job you need within your budget and timeline. If he has not already, he should also tell you if your goals are completely unrealistic. If you would really like to have a particular contractor do the work for you but his quote is not within your budget, ask him if he needs a show house. Show houses are properties that contractors agree to allow potential clients to come view their work in exchange for discounted services. However, because one contractor tells you that your budget is unrealistic, it is not always necessarily so. Nevertheless, if you call three or more contractors and you receive the same answer each time, it might be time to reevaluate your project.

If you have not seen the work of a contractor you are considering, ask him if he has a show house or location that will let you view his completed work. Then go look at it to make sure what the contractor does will fully meet your needs. Clarify how long it took the contractor to complete the job you view, and then compare it to the project he will be doing for you. Also, ask potential contractors how many other projects they will be working on while doing yours. Sometimes even the best contractors can overwhelm or overbook themselves before they even realize it. Asking them to clarify will not only give you the opportunity to know where you stand, but will help them do a mental check and balance before committing to a job they cannot fulfill.

Once you have found three contractors who can do the work within your budget and timeline, review their bids carefully. Be sure to do side by side comparisons. Are there any supplies or fees one contractor is offering to supply in his contract that another is not? Is one of the contractors offering to get the work done sooner than the other two?

Check the amount of labor each contractor promises to bring to the project. Do any of the contractors have a larger labor pool than the others? When speaking with the contractors, did you seem to click well with any of them over the others? These are all things to consider when locating a contractor.

See the Contracts section of Chapter 4: *A Legal Primer* for more information concerning contracts specifically.

HOME INSPECTORS

Home inspectors are individuals who, for a fee, can inspect a home for problems that may not be obvious to the average person. They are particularly valuable when you are considering purchasing a piece of property you intend to flip, and they are almost essential if you do not have a lot of construction knowledge. In fact, many lenders will actually require a report from a professional home inspector before they will approve a mortgage for a piece of property. A home inspector can help you determine if a potential property is a stable structure, or if the termites that have almost eaten the internal beams of the structure into sawdust will cost you any chance there might have been in reaping a profit from it.

A home inspector can also give you good information about the condition of the electrical wiring, roofing, drainage, and foundation. He can tell you if there are any gas leaks or the potential for any gas leaks, if there is a problem with insulation, and if condensation or climate is likely to have or has had an effect on the condition of the property. In short, he may sound like your archenemy when he is going through a home that you were rather looking forward to reconstructing, but he could be saving you lots of money and even more headaches.

If you can, find a home inspector who has been in the business for several years and who spent time as either a construction worker or contractor before becoming an inspector. These are the people who know property best. It is also important to find a home inspector who will be frank and candid with you. It is crucial that he tell you what is wrong with a potential investment, but it is equally essential that he also tell you whether the problem can be fixed, and what it is going to cost you. Just because an inspector finds problems with a property, it does not automatically mean that it is a bad investment. You should take into consideration the cost of the repairs with the value it will add to the property and the overall effect it will have on the worth of the property. It could very well be that, in the larger picture, fixing a problem, even though it may cost you several thousand dollars, will net you several thousand more in profits when you sell the house.

Look for someone who is personable yet professional, and who has preferably worked with investors. Let him know up front that you are looking at the investment potential of the property and that you are interested in the costs and time necessary to repair problems.

4

A LEGAL PRIMER

With the purchase of a new home comes the bureaucratic trail of paperwork. Without some background on what each document is and how it is important to the ownership process, it can be easy for a buyer to become frustrated and even discouraged. Fortunately, with a little bit of explanation and clarification, what seems to be mountainous obstacles of the home buying process can actually be quite easily shrunken to mere molehills.

Whenever possible, avoid attaining property under your own name. You are liable for any legal or tax issues that may arise when you operate under your own name. Instead, consider incorporating or forming a limited liability company to minimize the risks to your personal finances. Forming a business will also allow you to establish a separate credit file for your business, which will also somewhat protect your personal credit score should you ever stumble.

MORTGAGES

A mortgage, contrary to popular belief, is not actually the home loan itself. A mortgage is actually the written commitment placed on the new home by the new owner as collateral for repayment of the loan. If a new homeowner defaults on his loan, the house is given to the bank. When seeking a mortgage for a property you intend to flip, it is important to clarify whether the mortgage can be freely assumed. For those that can be, the transfer of property is simply a matter of taking over payments. Issues such as credit and closing costs are nonexistent when the existing mortgage can just be taken over by the new owner. However, many lenders are now requiring most mortgage contracts to contain clauses in them that require payment in full upon the sale of the property. In this situation, it is necessary for the buyer to secure a new mortgage, which also entails additional costs and requires a healthy credit score.

Sometimes mortgages themselves can be used as investment tools. When homeowners fall considerably behind on their mortgage payments, some banks will sell those defaulted mortgage payments to a third party for a payoff amount, because doing so is a smaller expense and less of a hassle then the foreclosure process. The third party who purchases the mortgages then becomes entitled to the lien on the property and may do with the mortgage as he or she chooses. Some will attempt to collect payment, some will negotiate with the homeowner to arrange a scenario very similar to that of landlord and tenant, and others will pursue the foreclosure in order to attempt to assume the property. It should be noted that while some investors earn their living exclusively from the purchase of mortgages, this is actually a very risky sort of investment.

There are several different types of rates and repayment types attached to home mortgage loans. Some are better than others are for specific uses, which we will discuss in a later chapter. For now, we will examine the various types of rates only.

Balloon Mortgages: Balloon mortgage loans allow you to make low payments for a short amount of time. The loan payments are structured in line with a traditional mortgage period such as 20, 25, or 30 years. However, the term length of the loan itself is much shorter than a regular mortgage. It is almost a home-buying equivalent to the buy now and pay only the interest for two years type of deals that car dealerships and furniture retailers often offer. Particularly since with a balloon mortgage, you are essentially only paying the interest for the term of the loan. At the end of the designated payment period, the entire loan comes due. These types of loans tend to be perfect for flipping, since the ideology behind flipping houses is to buy them, hold them only long enough to renovate, and then sell them for a profit. Because they allow investors to make smaller payments, balloon mortgage loans are not only a good choice for investors, but they also leave room for the loan to be paid off within a brief length of time without penalty.

Adjustable Mortgages: Adjustable mortgages have fluctuating interest rates. These types of loans usually have fixed rates for a period of time and then begin fluctuating to reflect current economic conditions. There is a limit set to the amount the bank can raise the interest, which is disclosed in the terms of the loan. An adjustable loan can be kind of a gamble in the world of flipping and can depend entirely on how long you plan to hold the property. Be sure you are clear on how long the fixed period is and whether there is a penalty for repaying the loan within the fixed period. If you intend to hold the property for any length of time, you will also want to make some sort of assessment of the economy and attempt to forecast, to the best of your ability, the outlook of the market for the length of time you intend to hold the property. Adjustable loans tend to lure you in with prime fixed rates, but you could be stuck with a bad rate if the market should take a downturn. If your fixed period ends while you are still holding the property, you may suddenly find yourself with high payments as a result.

Adjustable mortgages are typically not recommended for real estate investors of any type. The reason for this is that even though the payments remain steady, the interest being added to the back end of the loan is constantly adding to the overall amount you owe. Your fixed payments sometimes pay little more than the interest rate, which means the principle balance remains constant. Unless you can afford to pay more than your required monthly payment, it is possible for you to get caught in a cycle of paying to keep up the interest rate without ever chipping away the actual loan balance.

Fixed Mortgages: A fixed rate mortgage loan is a loan in which the interest rate and payment are set at the beginning of the loan and do not change. This loan is by far the easiest to understand and is great for buyers who intend to hold on to a piece of property for a considerable length of time, but it does not tend to be flip friendly, unless you intend to invest in a piece of property and hold it for several years while it appreciates in value.

Blanket Mortgages: Investors who purchase more than one property will often utilize a blanket mortgage. A blanket mortgage is simply a loan that covers multiple properties. The liens on each property are held collectively but released individually as each property is sold. Depending on the region in which you live and the lender, blanket mortgages are sometimes only offered to builders who are building on previously undeveloped land. However, blanket mortgages can occasionally be obtained by investors, particularly those who operate as corporations, for the purchase of multiple existing properties.

No matter which type of mortgage loan you choose, there will be essential documentation required by each one. Being prepared ahead of time makes the process go much more smoothly. In addition to the institution's loan application, you will need to provide your income tax returns for the past two or three years, depending on the individual lender's criteria, bank statements for the past three to six months, employment and income verification, an appraisal report, and an inspection report (if required). Some lenders will request that borrowers obtain copies of their credit reports themselves, while others will pull the major credit bureaus themselves for an additional fee. There may be other miscellaneous documentation required by individual financial institutions, but almost all lenders will require the above named documents.

Some financial institutions will offer loans with low (usually 5%) or no down payment to those buyers who meet certain credit criteria. Most lenders will require at least 10% down before they will agree to finance a mortgage. It is important to remember that even if you are able to secure a no or low down payment loan, there will still be fees for securing and underwriting the loan that may incur thousands of dollars. Therefore, it is very important to understand that you may be required to have access to some amount of cash, unless you are able to negotiate the displacement of the associated loan fees.

The two "Cs" — credit and cash — are the big determining factors when it comes to your negotiating power with financial institutions. The better your credit and the more cash you have behind you, the more lenders are going to be willing to wheel and deal. Do not assume that because the bank controls the loan disbursement that you have no room to negotiate. On the contrary, a bank is a business and just like all businesses, it is out to make money. Banks make money from customers, more specifically, good customers. If you have to show your purchasing power, you have negotiating power. Effectively convey to financial institutions that you are expecting to talk terms, and if they are not, you will take your money and their potential profit to another institution. The mortgage game is one where nerves of steel and a very strong backbone can pay off in a big way.

If your credit is not very good, your power of negotiation is considerably diminished. Although you may still be able to secure financing, your options will be dramatically more limited than those of someone with exceptional credit. This means you may be locked into terms that may not be the most desirable to you. A way to fight back from this and improve your credit in the process is to flip a few properties using those higher interest loans. As lenders begin to see that you have come through on your property repayments, they may be more willing to negotiate better loan terms with you. Otherwise, you are more or less locked into properties either with assumable mortgages or those that can be purchased on land contract. A land contract is primarily an agreement you come to with the owner in which he or she directly finances you. Some land contract terms are very similar to those of a mortgage with an initial down payment being paid to the owner and then monthly payments thereafter, until the property is paid off.

Some tips that can help you create an impressive picture of yourself to a lending officer, regardless of your credit situation, include:

- **Do your homework.** Have a project timeline and budget mapped out. If possible, support the final price you intend to ask for the house with information regarding the recent market prices and sales of comparable houses in the area. This information is available from a simple MLS lookup. If you do not have access in your area, have your realtor look it up for you. Have other useful information about the neighborhood ready to demonstrate why you believe it is worthwhile to invest in the particular area in which the property is located. Be prepared to show how the property will be reformed, as well as the profit you expect to earn from its rehabilitation.

- **Know the order of your financial affairs.** Lenders are not generally impressed by those asking for a mortgage loan when all of the other financial aspects of their life are a mess. Have your net worth detailed in a spreadsheet. Be prepared to show how much you are worth and from where that worth can be ascertained. Check your credit reports and bring them with you. Be prepared to discuss negative marks. If there is any information greater than seven years in age, write the bureaus to have it removed. Legally, after seven years, negative information must be removed from your credit report, if you request it. Also, if there are any debts on your report that are showing as unpaid that you have since paid, be prepared to bring receipts and, if possible, letters from the company in question confirming the debt has been settled. A negative mark on a credit report is not necessarily a deal ender by itself, if you can show that you have made efforts to correct it.

- **Have a business plan.** Even though you may not be starting a traditional business, it is still a business, nonetheless. Having a plan on paper that shows how you intend to earn and increase profits shows that you are undertaking your real estate venture very seriously. Lenders like consistency, and demonstrating to a loan officer that you have taken the time and put in the thought required to write a business plan suggests that you have given considerable thought to your real estate career, and it is not a passing whim.

- **Know your mortgage options and which one is best for you.** Be up front. Tell the lender why you would like a specific type of mortgage and how that would best serve the situation.

Loan amortization becomes crucial to this part of the process and can figure considerably into your eventual profits. A typical home loan has a duration of 30 years. However, with many lenders, it is possible to seek terms of 15, 20, or 25 years. Although the payments for these loans are significantly higher, they are paid off faster, thus significantly reducing the amount of interest that is paid on them.

If you are holding a piece of property solely for its appreciation value, then this can be a good option, because your ultimate financial goal is to sell the house at a considerable appreciation from the price at which you bought it. However, if you purchase a piece of investment property with the intention of holding it as a landlord in order to earn monthly profits from it, then a reduced loan term will pull from those profits, since you will be making a higher mortgage payment every month.

Assuming, however, that you purchase a piece of property in an up and coming neighborhood with the idea of selling it at a profit several years later, a reduced term could potentially earn you considerably higher profits. For instance, you will pay $310,000 ($210,000 in interest and $100,000 in principle) for a $100,000 home at a 7 perecent simple interest rate over a traditional term of 30 years. However, for that same house over a reduced 15-year term, you would pay $205,000 ($105,000 in interest and $100,000 in principle). In these terms, a house would need to appreciate to more than three times its purchase value before you would earn a profit from its sale through a 30-year loan. Whereas, the value of the property would only need to increase to twice its original worth, which is a feat that can be realized in some really hot neighborhoods in a matter of a few years, through a 15-year loan. Even if you plan to hold the property longer, you will still have saved $110,000, which could easily be used to purchase another property, and it makes any appreciation of the property value beyond the fifteen-year mark pure profit by paying off the property within fifteen years.

There is a certain risk involved in a reduced term loan versus a traditional 30-year loan. Primarily, your debt to spending ratio is considerably increased, which means that unless you have considerable cash flow already, it may be difficult to secure other loans or lines of credit when lenders see that you are already obligated to such a high mortgage payment. Therefore, even though you may be doing a good thing by paying off that particular property in only fifteen years, you may be somewhat stalling your business by limiting your ability to secure other properties. If you are just starting out or if you already have a lot of debt, your best option, regardless of profit impact, may be to go for the traditional 30-year term. Some investors always go for this option anyway, in order to keep their business going, and then they pay more than their minimum monthly payment in order to pay the loan off prematurely. It should be noted, however, that some lenders apply penalties to early pay offs. Before opting for a 30-year loan with the intentions of paying it off early, be sure to read the fine print, and ensure that you are not going to be stuck paying any penalties for prematurely paying off the loan.

DEEDS

The deed is simply the document of ownership to a piece of property. There are actually several different types of deeds. Warranty deeds are the most common types of deeds. A warranty deed states that a piece of property and all rights and responsibilities related to it belong exclusively to the holder of it. Quitclaim deeds are often used in situations in which there is some sort of split between joint owners of property or when one owner agrees to sell his share to the other. In signing over a quitclaim deed, an owner surrenders all rights in his share of the property. A quitclaim deed can most easily be remembered as a sort of property ownership resignation. When a homeowner encounters financial difficulties and is in danger of foreclosure, he can sometimes arrange to sign a deed in lieu of foreclosure, which is a form of voluntary repossession for property. By signing over the deed to the lender, the homeowner and the lender avoid the formal foreclosure process.

Although deeds can be and sometimes are freely handwritten, all deeds must contain certain information in order to be considered legal and binding. It must be written and declare the type of deed it is, it must declare the full names of all parties to the transaction and detail their roles exactly, and it must disclose what was exchanged or given by the grantee to the grantor for the title to the property. The plot map description of the property must be on the deed in exactly the same form as it appears in local records, the deed must be signed by both parties, and, in many localities, it must be witnessed by an authorized party, such as a notary public.

WARRANTY DEED

The warranty deed specifies that the seller fully owns the property and assumes responsibility for resolution in the event of any claims that may be made against it. Since a warranty deed is the closest document to a guarantee of property ownership, many lenders will insist on the procurement of a warranty deed as a precursor to the loan.

Warranty Deed

For and in consideration of _____, I have bargained and sold to _____ all that real property situated in _____ in the county of _____ and state of _____ bounded and described as follows: _____ *[legal description of real property]*.

I attest that I am legally within my rights in regard to the above named property to hereby dissolve and bequeath all rights, title, interest, profits, and rents to the above named buyer. I attest that in doing so, this property is free and clear of all liens, judgments, sales, taxes, restrictions, and encumbrances that may otherwise prevent the legal transference of said property.

[Signature of Seller]

_____

Witness my hand [and seal] this _____ day of _____*[month]*, _____*[year]*.

[Notary Public]

_____

[Witness]

_____

DEED OF SALE

A deed of sale is simply a document that is typically prepared by a seller and buyer once some sort of sale is negotiated. It simply states that the buyer has given the seller some type of compensation for the property and that the seller acknowledges that compensation as payment in exchange for ownership. A deed of sale is typically a good faith agreement from a seller to a buyer.

Deed of Sale

Deed made this _____ day of _____[month], _____[year], between _____, of _____, referred to as the grantor, and _____, of _____, referred to as the grantee.

The grantee is desirous of _____ and the grantor has agreed, in consideration of _____ dollars paid by the grantee, the receipt of which by the grantor is acknowledged, to grant to the grantee the property located at_____.

In consideration of _____ dollars *[or other consideration]* paid by the grantee to the grantor, the grantor grants to the grantee, his *[her]* heirs and assigns, full and free right and authority to _____.

The grantee covenants with the grantor that he [she], his [her] heirs, or assigns will _____.

In witness the grantor has signed [and seal] the day and year first written above. In the presence of _____.

_____

[Signature of grantor]

Notary Public

QUITCLAIM DEED

A quitclaim deed is a document in which an owner or joint owner relinquishes ownership of property. Quitclaim deeds are typically used in situations in which two or more people have owned a piece of property and ownership by any or all of the parties is being transferred due to dissolution of the coop or partnership. Divorces are a good example of when a quitclaim deed might be used.

Quitclaim Deed

For and in consideration of the property located at_____, in the county of _____ and state of _____ bounded and described as follows: _____ _____ *[legal description of real property].*

In consideration of the compensation of _____this quitclaim deed does serve to remit and release all ownership, interest, title, and rights by grantor _____ to the above stated property unto seller_____ whose current address is _____ .

Witness my hand [and seal] this ___day of _____*[month],* _____*[year].* This quitclaim deed is executed.

[Notary Public]

_____

[Acknowledgment of Seller]

_____

[Acknowledgment of Buyer]

_____

[Witness]

_____

SPECIAL DEEDS

Special deeds may be referred to by different names or titles from state to state, but they are all essentially deeds created for special circumstances and simply state that the current owner assumed the property under unique circumstances and has not made any changes, repairs, or improvements to the property while it was under his ownership. Foreclosures are an excellent example of when a special deed may come into play.

CONTRACTS

Although the two previous forms of paperwork, mortgages and deeds, are contracts, in this section, we will specifically address contracts that you may exchange with contractors you hire to do work on a property you intend to renovate. A good rule of thumb to apply to contracts is the old-fashioned, article-writing concept of who, what, where, why, when, and how plus one. The plus one is, of course, costs. Ensuring that a contract answers all of these questions plus costs is a good way of checking that all ground has been covered. However, construction contracts are frequently appended throughout a project, and the details can often times become hazy and expensive.

A major trap for most homeowners when hiring a contractor is assuming what is included in a contractor's services. It is a very good idea to have a contractor explain his proposal. Even though one contractor's bid might be a couple of hundred dollars more than another's, it could be because that contractor found some type of repair during his initial assessment that the other one did not find, and he included that service in his contract. In that particular case, those couple of hundred dollars in the initial costs could save you several hundred down the road. Equally, when a contractor adds in services that others do not, ask him why he feels that particular work is necessary in order to complete the job. Some contractors will occasionally throw in some additional work to beef up the proposal a bit and earn some extra money. When reviewing the breakdown of a contractor's proposal, ask him to explain any charges or fees you do not understand. He should be prepared to provide you with a clear explanation of all costs and fees. If he cannot, it should serve as a red flag. That contractor may not be as knowledgeable as he has attempted to make himself seem or he may just not have a good grasp on estimating costs, which could add up to a lot of unplanned add-ins and change orders for you. In addition to making sure the contract you sign details exactly what work will be done as well as what work will not be covered by the contract, it should also include:

- Total costs for the project including all labor and what supplies and permits will be included in the costs and who is responsible for obtaining them.

- Starting and ending dates as well as any other dates that are crucial to your timeline.

- A specific schedule for payment and a deadline by which the contract must be signed and work must begin in order for the contract to be valid.

- Stipulations for breach of contract penalties.

- Reasons and allowances for provisional changes to the contract, such as unforeseen problems and circumstances. The contract should detail that a change order should be submitted and improved before this type of work begins or becomes a part of the contractual obligation.

In addition, you should request that a contractor provide a list of all employees who will be working under him as well as what working hours he intends to maintain. A poorly designed contract without sufficient consideration of the details is not only confusing, but it can be costly. A good contract should act as a clarifying tool to both the homeowner and the contractor.

Many people assume that the first contract signed is the final document. However, in many cases, this is not so. Essentially, a contract is usually a live document that can be and is altered throughout the course of a project as unexpected issues that were not addressed in the original contract arise. A contract gives a contractor permission to do the work that is disclosed in it and only under the terms described, which means that a contract limits a contractor as much as it enables him. As he encounters work that either must be or ideally should be performed, the contractor must first consult his employer. Only after both parties have agreed that the new work should be done and it is put into writing as an addendum, usually called a change order, can the work legally be performed.

CHANGE ORDERS

A change order can also be issued to correct errors or eliminations in the original contract. For instance, if a contract for the services of a floor installer is based on 200 square feet of space and the room in which a floor is being laid is actually 260 square feet, a change order would need to be issued in order to compensate for the sixty square feet that is currently unaccounted for under the current contract terms. It is important to understand that in the vast majority of cases, it does not matter whether the original error in figuring the square feet was on behalf of the employer or the contractor. The fact of the matter is that there are 60 square feet for which the terms of the contract do not account to either party. Therefore, the contract must be changed in order to assign accountability for those 60 square feet to either one party or the other. The terms under which the change order is made are what is negotiable and they can be infinitely unique and varied.

To avoid the costs associated with multiple change orders, many people will actually write in stipulations that give the contractor some amount of leeway in making decisions and altering work before a change order must be sought. This gives the contractor some executive authority in exercising his expertise. However, it is important to keep in mind that this type of contractual arrangement is usually a form of convenience and may have some negative impact to your budget.

PAYMENT SCHEDULE

It is important for you to understand your contractor's payment schedule as well as the payment contingencies of the contract. For instance, some contractors include clauses in their contracts which state they will not move on to the next phase of project until payment for the current stage is received in full. This means that if your contractor completes phase I of a project and you are unable to pay him for that work for five days, he will cease work for those five days, rather than moving on to phase II. Although there really is not a standardized payment schedule to which all contractors abide, most of them usually operate on a three or four payment system. Two common breakdowns for the three-part system are 30%/30%/30% or 30%/50%/20%. With the four-part system, the breakdown is usually 50%/20%/20%/10% or 30%/30%/30%/10%.

These breakdowns are often negotiable, and you should not be surprised to see other payment systems and breakdowns depending on the particular contractor and the size of the job. We have hired a plumber who just requested a payment in full upon satisfactory completion of the job and an electrician who once simply asked for a 50% deposit and 50% upon completion. The first payment is usually considered some sort of deposit or good faith money. Some contractors will also ask for costs to purchase materials upfront. This is why the initial payment is significantly higher than other payments are. Other contracts prefer to break down their schedules more evenly and purchase materials as they are needed throughout the project. The second and third payments are often good faith money to demonstrate agreement between the contractor and yourself that you are satisfied with the work and the progress being made. The final payment is usually withheld until an inspection is passed and you give the final okay to the completed project.

It is very important, if you ever have the misfortune of finding yourself in a situation in which you are unhappy with a contractor's work, that you do not make the final payment to the contractor until the work is completed to your satisfaction. Once you have made the final payment, the contract is considered complete and, from a legal standpoint, it is widely considered your stamp of approval for the final project. If the need should arise to settle the dispute between the contractor and yourself in small claims court, one of the first questions an arbitrator or judge is going to ask you is why you made the final payment if you were dissatisfied with the work. Of course, if the problem that leads you to court is not discovered until after the contract has been settled, then the answer to that question will not carry as much weight. You will need simply to explain why you initially found the work satisfactory and then demonstrate what lead you to believe the subsequent problems were a direct result of errors on behalf the of the contractor. If, however, you are initially dissatisfied with the contractor's work and the finished project falls short of the expectations agreed upon in your contract, then you should withhold the final payment until the contractor makes the necessary corrections or you go to small claims court. It is crucial, though, to remember that either way, in small claims court, the burden of proof is on the plaintiff, not the defendant. If you sue the contractor, you must prove that the work he performed is not what was stipulated by your contract. If the contractor sues you, he must prove that he satisfactorily completed the project in accordance with the contract and that you were the one who fell short of the agreement. By taking a few necessary precautions when interviewing and hiring your contractors, you will hopefully never find yourself in this position. Mistakes and accidents do happen, though, so it is important to be properly informed and prepared when they do.

TIMELINE FOR COMPLETION

Besides ensuring that your timeline is included in your contract, it is important that you frequently check up on your contractor to check his progress. Communication is essential. At times, you may feel somewhat like a taskmaster, but it cannot be said enough that in real estate, time is money. Your budget and profit are relying on the completion of projects within their specified timelines. Although you will, at least once during your career (and probably several times), encounter situations that will force you to make minor adjustments to your timeline, you should still attempt to keep projects on task and budget. If you can, stipulate conditions of a project going significantly over time or budget in your contract. Placing a penalty in the contract, for instance, that calls for the reduction of the final payment by a certain percentage for every day it goes over the timeline or offering a bonus for work completed early or on time is a good way to keep your contractor motivated. Earning extra money or the prospect of losing it are both powerful motivators. If such a clause is included, it then becomes the duty of the contractor to disclose any additional time he may need to complete a project in a change order, as well as his reasons why.

Sample Contractor Agreement
SALES AGREEMENT

This agreement is made on _____[date], between _____[name of seller], of _____[address], _____[city], _____ County, _____[state] ("seller"), and _____[name of buyer], of _____[address], _____ [city], _____ County, _____[state] ("buyer").

SECTION ONE
Description of Services

The contractor shall perform the following services

_____

_____

_____On or before_____[date]

SECTION TWO
Consideration

Buyer shall accept and pay $_____ for the above named services.

SECTION THREE
Location of Services

Work shall be performed on the property located at _____ _____[address]

SECTION FOUR
Payment Schedule and Conditions

Buyer shall make payment for services based on the following schedule

30%	Commencement of Work
30%	Upon completion of 50% of work
40%	Upon satisfactory completion of all work

Contractor will be penalized $_____ per day for each day

SECTION FIVE
Independent Action

The contractor shall perform all duties assigned within contract at his/her discretion within reasonable means to complete the named services within the terms of this agreement. All changes, addendums, and alterations not expressly agreed upon within the terms of the agreement shall be submitted to employer in the form of a change order. This includes the acquisition of any materials not named herein, the employment of assistants or subcontractors not named herein, and the provision of equipment not named herein.

_____ *[signature, contractor]*

_____ *[signature, employer]*

SECTION SIX
Provisions

Equipment.

Contractor agrees to provide all equipment and tools necessary for completion of work and services.

Materials.

Contract will obtain and provide all materials necessary for completion of above named services.

Subcontractors/Employees/Assistants.

Contractor may, at his/her own discretion and expense, employ or subcontract assisting personnel for completion of work. Contractor assumes all expenses, responsibility, taxes, and wage liability for all subcontractors, employees, and assistants.

Insurance.

The contractor agrees to provide all applicable liability insurance for services performed. If the contractor should fail to maintain insurance, the contractor assumes all liability, accountability, and responsibility for any resulting fines, lawsuits, accidents, and claims resulting in association with his work or the work of any persons employed or subcontracted by him.

Invoices.

Contractor will provide written invoices to employer for all services performed.

Independent Contractor.

Contractor attests that he is an independent contractor and is not an employee or affiliate of any company or corporation not named within this contract.

_____ [contractor signature]

_____ [employer signature]

SECTION SEVEN
Right of Inspection

Employer shall have the right to inspect the services on completion and within _____ business days after delivery. Employer must give notice to seller of any claim for damages on account of condition, quality, or grade of the goods, and employer must specify the basis of the claim of employer in detail. The failure of employer to comply with these conditions shall constitute irrevocable acceptance of services by employer.

The parties have executed this agreement at _____ [designate place of execution] the day and year first above written.

_____

[Employer Signature]

_____

[Contractor Signature]

You should remember when writing your contracts that although you need to protect yourself and meet the needs of your business, you do not want to take advantage of your contractors. It is essential to build a reputation for yourself as being a fair and trustworthy business owner. You will probably need lots of contractor help during your career as an investor. Not only is it desirable to find contractors with whom you are comfortable and to form lasting relationships, but it can actually pay off for you in the end. Finding a contractor with whom you have a good rapport can be a way of ensuring that you always have someone to do quality work for you at a fair price and sometimes on very little notice. You will find that, like investors, many contractors have a healthy competition amongst themselves. They may compete against each other for business, but they are close friends and allies away from work. This means that they talk and often rely on each other's advice. If you become known as a business person who rips contractors off, then eventually no one will be too eager to work with you, whether you are nice to them or not.

TAXES

As with all money earned in the United States, the income you earn from flipping is subject to the various tax laws. If you deal in property, which is what real estate investors do, then the profits you earn from the sale of each property are subject to regular income tax. From the vantage of the IRS, if you are in the business of real estate, you can earn income from both the operation and sale of real estate, and you are taxed separately for both. Yes, even the federal government understands that real estate investing is a profitable business and a great way to earn money. The way to minimize the impact of either of these taxes is to offset your gains with expenses and losses. Of course, in order to be taxed for real estate operations, you must first hold a property long enough to operate it in any way. What this means is that taxes for the operation of property resulting in a capital gain are only incurred for property that is owned for a specific length of time. Since real estate tax laws are constantly changing, it is almost impossible to state what the specific period is, but it is typically six months or more. The good news about capital gains is that they are taxed at a much lower rate than the normal rate of income tax you will be required to pay for the sale of property. The bad news is that if you are in the business of buying and flipping, within a matter of weeks, you will not qualify for capital gains. According to the Revenue Reconciliation Act, you can deduct real estate losses from your income if your primary business is real estate. Expenses and repairs both qualify as losses and can be deducted from your earned income. Unfortunately, if you made the decision to dabble in real estate as a part-time venture, you will not enjoy the tax cushion of which full-time entrepreneurs can take advantage. If you decide to operate a property as a rental, you can utilize capital gains and losses. However, the bad news is that rental income is still considered income.

The 1031 Exchange law is another way in which many investors protect both their operating and selling incomes. The 1031 Exchange allows you to reinvest your profits from the sale of one property into the purchase of another property or properties without first being taxed on them, provided that you predetermine properties of interest within six weeks of selling the initial property, purchase one of those properties of interest within six months, and continuously earn a profit from the sale of your properties. As long as you continuously do this following the 1031 Exchange guidelines, your profits remain free of immediate taxation. This allows you, as an investor, to build your net worth.

Another advantage many investors use to maximize their income and minimize taxation is the small down payment option. Real estate down payments are not tax deductible. Instead, it is the purchase price of a piece of property that becomes the bar for taxation. Putting up a lower down payment, though, means higher monthly mortgage payments and higher monthly mortgage payments do directly affect your bottom line. This means that lower down payments and higher monthly mortgage payments can help lower your taxes by decreasing your actual income earned. In this method, it really comes down to whether you would prefer to immediately have cash in hand or temporarily inventory it within the property.

Interest rates on both equity lines of credit and mortgage loans are tax deductible, but the principle balances themselves are not. It is also important to note that the tax-deductible portion of the interest on equity lines of credit typically has a cap that directly relates to a debt to home value ratio of the loan. If you care to live in the properties in which you invest for at least three years, you can keep the profits from the sale of your property up to $500,000. The tax law that grants this easement is not a real estate or investment law at all. It is the federal government's own tax incentive to encourage home ownership. However, you must live in the property for at least two years, and there are some rules and restrictions to this law, so it is a good idea to consult your accountant.

5

THE ISSUE OF FINANCING

Financing is, of course, the biggest obstacle to the realization of the dreams of many would be investors. In order to acquire property, you have to have financing and seeking it out can be daunting. Although there are programs out there that maintain that you can get rich with no money down and no credit, that is not a realistic goal for many. There are certain prerequisites to obtaining property that you are going to need to fulfill.

You are going to need a down payment. The good news is that, currently, lenders are requiring less and less of a down payment to finance property. It is quite realistic to obtain most property with 5% down. However, the fact of the matter is, without a down payment to back you up, most lenders are not going to be apt to believe that you are financially prepared for purchasing property. Remember that lenders are primarily concerned with the prospect of getting their money back.

Showing them that purchasing a piece of real estate is important enough to you that you are willing to commit a substantial amount of your own hard earned money toward it speaks volumes. If you do not have cash now, start saving or explore alternative options for raising cash, such a withdrawal from your 401K or an equity line of credit on your current home if you own one.

Your credit will need to be decent. Notice the word used was not "excellent." There was a time when only impeccable credit would get you a house. These days, there are enough finance companies that work with slow or problem credit that, unless you are a complete deadbeat, you will be able to obtain a home loan. You may not be able to get the most desirable interest rate, but you will still be able to get the loan. You will find fewer and fewer lenders looking for justification for a late payment from three years ago, but all lenders are still going to want to know why there are some things on your report that you never paid. So, know what is on your credit report and be prepared to answer questions. If your credit is questionable now, save for a couple of years while you focus on cleaning up your act, so that you can go to a lender in a year or two and show him or her that you have made a concentrated effort to get your financial matters in line. It is easier for lenders to take you seriously when you can demonstrate a serious effort on your behalf.

Assess what you can afford. Of course, everyone starts out with big dreams. The reality is that you are going to have to establish a base line to act as your starting point. In order to do this, you are going to need to take a good hard look at your net worth. What assets do you have? In addition, how much would you get for them if you converted them to cash? Then, reexamine your paycheck. Are you living from pay period to pay period, or do you bring home enough money to stash a little extra here and there? If you are already making paychecks stretch and you are serious about becoming a real estate investor, this might be a good time to think about paring down and simplifying your lifestyle in order to make some room to begin saving. Sometimes that requires a rather large commitment.

If you are already struggling every month to meet your mortgage payment, how do you expect to be able to juggle a second one, even for a short period? In that case, maybe your first move in real estate should be the sell of your current home to something smaller and more affordable, or perhaps you might want to consider trading your current home to purchase your first flip and living in it while you renovate. If, however, you could build a considerable savings in a rather short time by cutting out your daily cup of Starbucks, substituting it with $.50 coffee from the local gas station, or hitting the shopping mall less often, you might want to begin there. Although you may only be able to afford to flip starter homes in a lower price range in the beginning, you will eventually be able to build to larger properties as your earnings grow.

FINDING YOUR SOURCE

Once you have taken an honest look at where you stand, you will need to find a source for your financing. Lender choices are diverse and varied, but finding the right type of lender can be pivotal, so give the decision the time and consideration it deserves. First, ask yourself what your flipping style is going to be. Are you going focus your efforts on dealing, or are you going to be a retailer? If you want to give it a go as a dealer, then the details of the lender are less important, since you will not actually be assuming property. You may even think about a simple line of credit, rather than a full-fledged mortgage, since you will never actually be making payments.

If your decision is to be a retailer, how long do you intend to hold your property? If you are only going to be holding it for month or two, then you might want to take advantage of a loan type that allows for smaller or interest owner payments in the early stages, such as a balloon loan. This allows you to hold the property briefly while only incurring a small amount of out-of-pocket costs toward your mortgage.

If you are going to be holding the property for several months or even years, then mortgage interest rates and types become essential, and you are going to want to examine several different types of loans and lenders to determine your best option.

BROKERS AND DIRECT LENDERS

First, you will want to distinguish between mortgage lenders and mortgage brokers. Brokers are middlemen. They are given a lender's criteria and loan availability, and they set out to find consumers who fit those stipulations. Once they do, the broker matches the borrower to the lender. The primary drawback to brokers is that middlemen charge fees and you will, more often than not, get stuck paying the fee. However, a broker also has access to a lot of different lenders and many different types of loans. What this means is that they can take your application, assess your needs, and shop you to multiple lenders. Since brokers make their money by making viable consumer to lender connections, they are particularly talented at sprucing up your loan application and selling you, as a buyer, to lenders. Sometimes, particularly if your credit is less than stellar or you have some questionable financial history, this can make those intermediary fees well worthwhile, despite initial impressions. However, if you have exceptional credit and quite a bit of cash flow, it might pay if you skip the intermediary and go directly to lenders.

Direct lender programs are usually considerably more limited in nature than that of brokers, primarily because lenders can only offer you their own products. If they do not have a loan to fit your needs, then they cannot simply take your application and pass it on to the next lender. However, the costs and interest rates of loans obtained directly through lenders are often significantly less than those obtained through brokers, because there is no mark up involved. If you do your homework and know that a lender offers the type of loan you need and you are either particularly adept at selling yourself or your credit and financial records are able to speak volumes in themselves, a direct lender can be a more money saving, not to mention somewhat speedier, option than brokers.

PROPERTY OWNERS

Sometimes the best financing sources are property owners themselves. Land contracts are common financing terms that are usually arranged directly between a property owner and a buyer. A land contract is simply a contractual agreement for a buyer to purchase a property directly from an owner. Like a mortgage, they often involve an initial down payment followed by monthly payments to the owner and, unlike a rental, the property is deeded to the buyer. The lien is held by the owner until the agreed upon price of the property is paid in full. For a seller who already outright owns the property, land contracts are a way to turn a piece of property into monthly cash flow. For a buyer with less than perfect credit, a land contract is often an alternative path that leads to home ownership when it would otherwise be unreachable. Land contracts are particularly viable options for property that needs a considerable amount of work and may be difficult to sell on the traditional market, and they allow the buyer to begin making improvements immediately. Since you are only indebted to the original owner for the amount of the original contract, any subsequent earnings you make from the sell of the property are yours.

Owner financed property also offers buyers certain perks that actually supersede traditional financing. For instance, chances are that if you are utilizing seller financing, you are assuming a loan, which means that you do not incur the typical closing costs, loan origination fees, inspection costs, etc. This means that owner financed transactions allow for both the buyer and the seller to walk away from the table with more money in their pockets.

One potential drawback to owner financing, however, is that it may not necessarily improve your credit. Since most of these agreements are held strictly between the seller and the buyer, chances are that the owner is not experienced in reporting to credit bureaus. Unless you are assuming the mortgage, which is essentially taking over the existing mortgage, this means that your payments will not be recorded with the major credit bureaus. In fact, no one in the financial world other than yourself and the seller will ever even know or care that you are making the monthly payments on time. The upside to this, of course, is that if you should happen to default on the loan, it will not be reflected in your credit score, as the owner's sole recourse will be to resell the property to recoup lost money.

PRIVATE INVESTORS

A much rarer but viable option as a financing source can be a private investor. There are private individuals and companies that are willing to put up the money for an investment in exchange for a share of profits. If you are a particularly good salesperson and you feel you have a foolproof plan if only can get the financial backing, you may want to consider approaching a private investor. If you are unsure where to start, place an advertisement in your local classified ads. Some people who are willing to invest and have the money to do so simply have not done it, because they have not found the right opportunity. In these cases, it becomes your job to convince them that you have the key to turning their money into even more money.

If your credit is less than perfect and traditional lenders who are willing to give you a home loan are few and far between, you might want specifically to search out properties with assumable mortgages. Your potential field of play is going to be significantly narrowed through this approach, but it is an option and one that ties nicely into flipping, since most assumable mortgages are at least twenty years old or older. This means that, unless it has been extraordinarily well maintained, the property you acquire through an assumed mortgage is going to be automatically right for flipping.

It would not be very serving or informative to create an

entire book about earning fast profits in real estate without addressing the topic of credit repair. Most people have seen the many advertisements that promise a successful career in real estate, even for those with no or less than perfect credit. These claims are not false. If you have little or no credit or if you credit rating is less than stellar, it is possible to break into the business. Of course, the reality to that option is that there is a catch. In all likelihood, you are going to need some amount of cash, probably several thousand dollars, in order to get started. It does not matter what your source for this cash may be. You may even borrow it from friends or relatives if necessary. The point is that it is possible to obtain and flip your first property using cash. However, if you intend to buy and flip properties in a continuous chain, it will be impossible to ignore a poor credit history. Although buying and selling properties can actually improve your credit rating, you still may have to address other issues from your past and bide some time before your credit rating actually improves to a level that will begin to pay off in lower interest rates and more loan options.

Be sure to obtain copies of your credit report. Federal law now mandates that everyone be entitled to one free report per year. All three of the major bureaus will provide your report to you online after you verify some personal information. Once you receive your report, review it for errors or inaccuracies. Bankruptcies may appear on your bureau for up to ten years. Other negative marks can be reported for up to seven. After seven years, you can write to any credit bureau still reporting them and ask to have them removed. Remember that having a negative remark removed from your credit bureau simply means that it will no longer be reported. It does not necessarily mean that you no longer owe the debt. Different states have varying laws regarding the statute of limitations on closed and open-ended debts.

If you find any information on your credit report that is inaccurate, by law, you may write the credit bureau to dispute the debt. They have thirty days to respond. If they do not, you can legally ask them to remove the negative mark from your report. If there are balances being reported as unpaid that you know that you have settled, advise the bureau that you have settled the debt. Chances are that the bureau is either going to ask you to provide proof that you have paid the debt or tell you that you must contact the creditor in question and have them provide a letter of acknowledgment that the debt has been settled.

Although it will not improve your actual credit score, it is always a good idea to prepare letters of explanation for any negative marks or periods during which your credit was somewhat questionable. Sometimes lenders will consider these types of explanations. You should have good reasoning behind them and back up your claims of exception by showing that you have since taken verifiable steps to improve your financial and credit situation.

Private investors are also particularly good candidates if you are looking for a brains and brawn type of partnership. If you are particularly adept at the physical aspects of rehabbing property, you have a selling point to offer potential investors. The first question of any investor is going to be, "What am I going to get out of the deal?" If you can say to them, "With your money, I will turn a $120,000 piece of property into a $170,000 piece of property within six weeks (assuming you split the profits evenly) and will earn both of us a $25,000 profit," you can pinpoint experience to back up your claim, and potential investors will be more willing to listen. Even if you lack actual DIY experience but are a particularly talented negotiator and project manager, for example, you still have a particularly strong bargaining tool. Many investors love the idea of being able to turn their money into a considerable profit without having to do anything. Offering them a situation in which you will earn your share of the profit by doing all of the work is a temptation few will be able to decline.

PARTNERSHIPS

Partnerships are a great way to overcome financial issues, particularly if one of you has experience in construction or renovation, and the other has the finances. Your partnership opens the door for you to form a corporation. One of you can handle the financial and administrative aspects of the company, while the other manages the refurbishing projects. Not only will this allow both partners to maximize his or her skills, but it also provides the opportunity for you to move projects along more speedily, because each of you can focus more exclusively on your agreed upon duties.

The downside to a partnership, of course, is that your decisions will not be exclusively yours. They will be made dually. If the person with whom you form your partnership is of a like mind, then you probably will not find this the least bit detrimental the majority of the time. However, it is definitely something to which you will want to give fair consideration. It is also important that the person with whom you form partnership is someone you trust completely and that you are confident that he or she trusts you. A partnership cannot be productive if the parties involved do not have confidence in each other.

YOUR MONEY OR THEIRS?

There is no shortage of real estate gurus offering the secret to no money down real estate on late night infomercials. There are very few doors through which one can assume property without using any of his own money. If you do not plan to assume the property, virtually your only option is to do a double closing. This is different from a simultaneous closing, because all involved parties are in the same room, and all business is conducted at one time. In other words, your seller knows you are immediately reselling for a profit, and your buyer realizes that they probably could have gotten a better deal. In the end, you avoid paying any closing costs, because the investor to whom you sell to is the only person who brings cash to the closing. You may not exactly be helping your reputation in the business, since there is a high risk that the other two parties may leave the table feeling as though they were somewhat cheated, although what you have done was perfectly legal. On the side of caution, you will need to make sure that the deed you sign does not have a seasoning clause. If there is, then you must hold the property in your name for the specified period of time before transferring it. In this case, a double closing is not an option, and there is no way to deal the property to another investor without paying the closing costs out of your own pocket.

If you plan to assume the property in order to renovate and flip, you have two realistic options. Your first choice is to arrange with the owner of the property to sell to you on land contract. This type of deal is exclusively between the seller and the buyer, which means the terms are whatever the both of you can agree upon, as long as they do not conflict with any stipulations of the lender and the seller does not own the property outright. Your second option is to locate a seller who has an assumable mortgage loan, and simply assume the payments of the existing mortgage. There will still be closing fees in the sale, but you may be able to negotiate with the seller to put the money up for the closing fees and finance them to you.

Although many would defend the numerous creative options, wise investors will be weary of them. Not only do many of them walk a fine line between legal and illegal, but also they are somewhat questionable from an ethical standpoint. If you are unconcerned with the type of reputation you build as a businessperson as long as you earn a profit, then you may not care about ethics as long as legalities are covered. In that case, you can rest assured that many of the alternative methods frequently touted as "no money down" are perfectly legal, if done correctly.

Since the most popular, no money down method, the double closing, has already been covered in another section, we will not review it again here. Another popular way of purchasing property without cash is the dynamic duo method. In this method, two investors, acting as partners, often unbeknownst to the seller and lender, arrange to purchase the property for a significantly lower price than market value. That partner then, in turn, sells the property to the other partner at market price. The difference between the original purchase price and the final selling price becomes the profit. The method is similar to a double closing, except the two investors are working together, which means they can purchase and sell for a greater difference than a dealer who is simply working a double closing. Like traditional double closings, it is legal, as long as the market price of the house has not been intentionally over-inflated, and the two investors are not required to disclose their relationship unless they are asked. If asked, though, they should be upfront about their partnership.

Although over-inflation is a common practice sometimes exercised by buyers and sellers without discovery or penalty, it is illegal. Over-inflation is simply where the market value of a house is inflated in order to convince the lender to finance unknowingly the full purchase price. During the closing, the buyer gives the seller a down payment that the buyer then returns to the seller after the closing, because it has been covered in the amount of the loan. You should know that this is a form of fraud, and if you are caught, you could incur considerable fines and a rather lengthy prison term.

In simple terms, use your conscience as your guide. If you feel as though you are being sneaky or conducting shady business under the table, you probably are. In that case, even though what you are doing may not necessarily be illegal, it may be unethical. Think carefully through each step of what you are doing. Is anything or anyone being misrepresented? If the answer is no, then you have simply tapped into a method for making money. Welcome to the world of Capitalism!

If you already own a property and have any equity in it, you can always apply for a home equity line of credit.

CLOSINGS

Before the actual closing takes place, several prerequisite activities usually must take place. The most crucial item that is usually required is a title search. The title search verifies that the seller actually has the right to sell the property, and there are no serious liens or stipulations preventing the house from being sold. You can hire a company to do this search for you, or you can do it yourself. A title search is usually done at the county clerk and involves a checklist of details for which you should look:

1. Unpaid fees or taxes. This can include anything from property taxes all the way up to waste removal charges. If there are unpaid expenses against a piece of property, someone is going to have to pay them before the title can be transferred.

2. Bankruptcy petitions. Just because there is a bankruptcy petition attached to a property does not mean that the title is not marketable. If the property was included as part of bankruptcy and there is legal documentation stipulating that it was reaffirmed in the case, it means the property was not included in the bankruptcy. A seller should be able to show you documented proof of a reaffirmation. All reaffirmations are required to be put in writing and submitting to the bankruptcy court for approval. If this was not done, the property was not reaffirmed, and it is either being withheld from the bankruptcy, which is illegal, or it was not reaffirmed and is of questionable ownership.

3. Determine if there are any unbridged or unexplained blanks in the trail of ownership. If there is, then it is important to resolve the ownership of those years. Otherwise, future ownership could be questionable and messy.

Once you conduct the title search and establish any unclear or unresolved issues, contact the appropriate parties for either payoff or documentation information. Be sure to get receipts for anything you pay, so if it comes up in the course of preparing for the closing, you can show that the charges have been paid.

Title companies usually conduct closings. In addition to preparing the necessary documentation, they will also often attempt to sell you title insurance. Title insurance protects you from anyone coming out of the woodwork to lay claim to the property. Even if the claimant turns out to be valid, title insurance entitles you to any damages or expenses you may have incurred in the process. The worth of title insurance is directly relative to the amount of money you have or will be investing in the property. Less money coming out of your pocket means a smaller need to purchase title insurance. In general, title insurance is not mandatory for flipping, but if you are going to hold a property or have it for several months, it is a good idea to give title insurance fair consideration.

The final task that usually must be completed before the actual closing is a home inspection. Home inspections generally cost approximately $200, and the costs can sometimes be deferred to the seller as part of a contingency clause in the initial offer. Professional inspectors are a good idea for many reasons; namely, they can help identify any costly flaws that a piece of property might have before you assume ownership and discover them at a considerable cost to your budget and timeline.

Once all of the preliminary tasks are completed, the actual signing will take place between the buyer, the seller, and the closing agent. Although all parties are involved, it is important to understand that not everyone is always in the room at the same time. The signing involves the payment of the closing costs and the down payment, signing loan documents, and the exchange of the deed. If you are acting as a dealer, you will have a double closing. In the first closing, you will purchase the property. In the second closing, you will sell the property. Although it is technically two separate transactions, they can be, and often are, done at the same time and in the same room. However, for ethical reasons, you might want to consider conducting them back to back in separate rooms.

6

FHA/VA LOANS

T wo specific loan programs are set up by the federal government to encourage home buying to prospective homebuyers who otherwise might not be able to afford a new home: first-time homebuyers and veterans of the armed forces. These loans make the dream of home ownership possible for those who would have otherwise been unable to purchase by providing financing with very small down payments and guarantor insured loans. The FHA also offers a loan specifically targeted to investors who plan to reside in property while renovating it.

The 203(k) loan is a federal loan program that allows buyers to borrow money to finance a piece of property, plus the refinancing costs. Often, a down payment of only 3% is required with the remaining 97% of the home financed. The total loan amount can be 110% of the value of the property or the total rehab costs, whichever is less. FHA loans are obtained through traditional FHA approved mortgage lenders.

- Buyers are first subject to the lender's credit criteria. Some FHA approved lenders do offer sub prime loans for those with less than perfect credit. It is important to find a lender that can offer a program that best suits your needs.

- On the mortgage application, buyers should specify that they are seeking a 203(k) loan. Additionally, a proposal must be submitted that details the work that will be performed on the property. All repairs must be detailed and estimates of the costs must be included.

- The property is appraised to determine the post renovation value of the property in order to ensure that the total loan, including the costs of repairs, will not be significantly more than what it will ultimately be worth, even once it is restored to retail condition.

- The loan is underwritten for the asking price of the property, the estimated repair costs, an additional 10%-20% for unplanned or unexpected expenses, and the closing costs.

- Upon closing, the seller is paid the amount of the purchasing price and the remaining funds are placed into an escrow account for repairs.

- Funds from the escrow account are distributed directly to the contractor with 10% of the total of each job being held back until the work is completed.

There are a couple of additional facts that are good to know about 203(k) loans. First, they can be sought for either single-family or multiple unit dwellings. However, the number of units in the multifamily dwelling cannot exceed four. Condominiums are also eligible for the 203(k) loan program. FHA funded improvements must be restricted to the inside of the unit, and the building must either be owner occupied or held by a nonprofit organization. Condominium 203(k)s can involve more than four units but cannot exceed more than four units per building. Likewise, single-family homes can be converted to multiple family homes using a 203(k), but the new multiple family dwelling cannot exceed four units.

There is a $5000 minimum for eligible repairs. Eligible repairs are defined as the disposal of health or safety hazards, structural repairs, updates, exterior remodeling, replacement of outdated or nonworking systems (plumbing, heating, electrical, etc.), flooring and carpeting, roofing, drainage (including gutters and downspouts), landscaping and general land improvements, and the addition of handicap accessible facilities. All work must begin within 30 days of closing, may not stop for more than 30 consecutive days, and must be completed within six months of the original start date. If the buyer fails to meet the stipulations regarding rehabilitation, the lender may revoke the rehabilitation funds and apply them to the principle of the mortgage.

A professional contractor is not required to do the work under the current guidelines of the FHA program. However, a homeowner doing his or her own improvements must follow all the same procedures, such as writing up a formal job proposal for work to be done in order to withdraw funds from the escrow account. All work done by a homeowner is also subject to meeting FHA guidelines as well as local codes.

It is also important to understand that doing your own work under a 203(k) program in order to save money only pays in a way that frees up more funds for improvements. Leftover funds upon completion of the renovation are not returned to the homeowner. Any remaining funds can be applied to reduce the amount of the mortgage principle, but monthly payments will not change or be affected by this.

Although the 203(k) program is ideal for investing, investors acting solely in the name of property improvement are not permitted to participate in the program. The program is intended for buyers who intend to renovate property, which is why one of the guidelines of an FHA loan is that the property is owner-occupied. However, there are no federal restrictions preventing the occupant from selling the home after the renovations are completed. It is important, though, to clarify any seasoning guidelines the lender may have concerning the mortgage loan. There are also guidelines regarding how many properties a homeowner can have in the immediate area. Currently, the stipulations are that a buyer may not own more than seven units within a two-block radius. It is important to understand that in a multifamily dwelling, each apartment or condominium is considered a unit. Therefore, if you own two four-unit buildings within a two block radius, you exceed the seven-unit maximum and cannot qualify for a 203(k) loan.

In general, the 203(k) program is ideal for those who are looking for that first flip, have not purchased a home in a few years, and are considering living in the property for a while. If you want to explore the dealer side of flipping or if you already frequently buy or sell property, the FHA program is probably not the best fit for your needs.

There are also special loan programs to assist military veterans in purchasing a home. Much like the 203(k) loan, these programs offer government approved, no down payment options and have lower interest rates than traditional loans for veterans with fair or poor credit. In order to qualify, a veteran must have been honorably discharged from a branch of the U.S. Military and meet certain credit related criteria.

7

FINDING PROPERTY THAT IS PRIME FOR FLIPPING

O nce you familiarize yourself with the generalized process of house flipping, the players involved in it, and the documents you will be frequently signing, it is time to start looking for property. Locating property prime for investing requires a combination of instinct and science. First, you will need to find an in.

FINDING AN "IN"

As we reviewed in previous sections, having connections in the world of real estate is not only an advantage, it is critical to your success. It is important to build yourself a network of other investors and real estate professionals. First, introduce yourself as a buyer in the market and find an agent. Tell the agent that you intend to flip the house. A good agent will be able to put you in touch with others who may benefit from the connection. After some time, you will become familiar with other investors in the area as well. Although these people will sometimes be your competition, it is important to view them as potential helpers as well. Sometimes you will encounter a property or opportunity that is not right for your investment style, but may be perfect for a fellow investor with whom you are familiar. That same investor may eventually find himself in a similar situation with you in mind sometime in the future. View your competition as friendly, not hostile.

Auctions are another great way to find potential flipping property while familiarizing yourself with the local investment players and their hierarchy. After attending a few auctions, you will know who the power players are and have an idea of what it will take to survive in your local investment scene. You will also know what it will take to secure properties to flip in your area and how far your dollar will go. Do not become so involved in your observations, though, that you forget to mingle. Striking up a casual conversation in a setting as informal as an auction is a great way to begin forming your network. It can also be a good way to get to know some of the lawyers and accountants in your area who specialize in real estate.

Good old-fashioned newspaper classifieds can also be a great way to get your foot in the door. Look for classified ads that use taglines such as "We Buy Ugly Houses" or "Cash Now for Your Homes." Chances are, these are investors like you who are fishing for houses. Call the numbers and ask questions. Introduce yourself. You may initially be greeted with a bit of repressed hostility, but you just might make a friend who can provide you with some invaluable insight. When you feel the time is right, go fishing yourself by running a few ads of your own. You will get some curious inquiries, but you also just may convince that one homeowner who is desperate to unload a potential gem to sell to you at the right price.

Join a professional organization and attend a convention. Conventions and seminars are a great way to begin networking. Not only can you meet others in the business, but also you often get the opportunity to hear some of the most successful members of the community speak on what helped them succeed as well as what did not. The National Association of Real Estate Investors (NAREI), for instance, is an organization that offers the assistance of mentors, as well as educational opportunities and workshops to its members. Making friends within an organization of like-minded professionals is not only beneficial, but it can be profitable.

Advertise. Let people know that you are looking for properties in which to invest, in order to lead potential sellers to you. Place an advertisement in the classified section of your local periodical stating that you are an investor looking to buy property. Have business cards printed up and capitalize on every opportunity to pass them out or display them. Begin taking contact information from local For Sale signs in the area and directly contacting the selling agent. Speak with him or her about your goals. Most agents are motivated by potential clients and good ones are great informational resources.

Sponsor a local youth athletic team in a community recreation league and advertise in tournament books. This sounds rather trite, but it actually has far-reaching subliminal impact and is usually a somewhat inexpensive marketing ploy, typically less than $200. People may not necessarily realize that they are registering your business name every time they see it screen-printed across the jerseys of the team you sponsor, but when the time comes for them to utilize your services, they will often recall the name of the business that sponsored "the team with the purple shirts." In a way, this type of advertising works very much in the same way as paraphernalia for political campaigning, but research has proven that when voters know nothing about the candidates vying for a specific political office, they will cast their vote based on name recognition. Simply put, people choose what they know. Similarly, community members may not know that much about real estate, but if they spend twelve weekends in the spring and fall looking at your name splashed across the shirts of local youth and in the pages of tournament books as they try to figure out whether Junior's team is going to make it to the semifinals, they will know your name when the need arises. This greatly increases the chance of their calling you versus a random business name they pull out of the yellow pages.

Finding your first property is typically the most difficult. However, once you find yourself a way in and establish your team of professionals and contractors, your success is completely in your hands. You are limited only by the restrictions you place upon yourself.

IDENTIFYING NEIGHBORHOODS OF OPPORTUNITY

Although when you first begin to consider a career in real estate flipping, a specific neighborhood may immediately pop into your mind, choosing an area in which to focus is not always as obvious as it seems. Chances are, many of the hot neighborhoods in your area that are currently experiencing a renaissance of some sort are probably already overflowing with investors. In such cases, it may pay off more in the long run for you to do some research in order to determine what area may become the next new "it" neighborhood, and focus your efforts there. Investment properties are probably going to be costly in an area that is popular, and even retail buyers, who would otherwise prefer a home that is in move-in condition, may be willing to compete for a fixer upper for the opportunity to live in a neighborhood that they might not otherwise be able to afford.

In choosing a neighborhood to focus your flipping efforts, every beginning investor is faced with the problem of whether to buy the best house in the worst neighborhood or the worst house in the best neighborhood. Either could be the correct answer, depending on the situation. It is true that the more undesirable the neighborhood is, the smaller your potential buyers market will be. Quite simply, fewer people are willing to take risks for even the best house in a neighborhood notorious for crime, poor schools, or mostly rundown homes. However, if that neighborhood happens to be going through somewhat of renaissance, people may be more willing to take the chance in exchange for the opportunity to get in on the ground floor of a boom that promises to explode the value of the property within a few years. Therefore, the best bet for locating a neighborhood ideal for flipping homes is to locate an older neighborhood in town that is on the verge of rebirth. You can determine this, not merely by following home sales and property notices in the area, but just by following the development trends. If you begin to notice a fair amount of new retail or commercial businesses appearing in the area, that may be a good sign that the economy of that neighborhood is on the rise. Pay attention to local news features or stories that announce plans for new shopping centers, restaurants, or entertainment complexes.

If you do not already have a subscription to the local newspaper, get one. Checking the classified section should become a daily routine. In addition to checking the advertisements of homes for sale, you should also read the public notices. Public notices will include bankruptcy, foreclosure, and auction notices.

Take a drive. Drive around potential neighborhoods and pay attention to the general upkeep of homes in the area. Pay attention to the cars parked in the driveways or on the streets. Are they newer or older? If you are driving around during a business day, does there seem to be an unusual number of cars parked at their homes? Evaluate the neighborhood for its proximity to places of convenience such as gas stations or grocery stores. Search for other selling points for the area such as mature trees, wooded lots, etc. Make a mental note of the type of people you see out and about. Does the neighborhood appear to consist primarily of younger families, empty nesters, or young professionals? This will be your market demographic when its time for you to sell. As you peruse prospective neighborhoods, make a mental note if there seems to be an unusually high number of For Sale signs in the neighborhood. This could be a red flag for some sort of underlying issue in the neighborhood and may warrant further investigation.

Once you narrow your neighborhood search down to a couple prospective locales, start regularly checking the MLS ads for those areas. The Multiple Listing Service is a database of all properties for sale in a geographic region that is specifically targeted to real estate professionals. The MLS contains such information as square footage, a breakdown of room sizes, property tax information, annual homeowner's fees (if applicable), school district, and condition of the property. The MLS database will help you create a comparative foundation for what houses are selling for in the area and how condition is affecting selling costs. It can also help you establish a base for how long houses are generally staying on the market before being sold, which is important when each month your property goes unsold is costing you another mortgage payment. One aspect of MLS worth mentioning, however, is that in some cities, the MLS database is freely accessible to anyone with an internet connection while in other cities some of the information is restricted to real estate professionals. If you live in a city that does the latter, you will need to have your agent provide you with regular information from the MLS.

It is worth addressing the fact that, although some investors do not restrict their business to a single neighborhood or even city, it is not recommended that you begin your career on a national or international level. Conducting multiple and continuous real estate transactions across state lines requires a certain level of skill, experience, and expertise that requires a seasoned professional with a great staff and an even better attorney, because you are no longer dealing exclusively with the laws of one state, but many. Expanding to an international scale is something that should be considered very carefully. Although you will see many advertisements promising cheap real estate in foreign countries, it is important to remember that it's just as important to be familiar with the area in which you wish to buy in a another country as it is in your own. This means that, before you even begin to consider purchasing property in a foreign land, you will probably need to take multiple scouting trips, which, depending on the country in which you are considering investing, can become rather expensive very quickly. Once you determine that you would like to own property in that country, you will also need to familiarize yourself with the real estate laws of that country. This often involves a lot of bureaucratic red tape that is best and most efficiently dealt with by hiring an attorney licensed to practice in that country. Finally, once you own a home or piece of land in a foreign country, before you even begin any type of work on it, you will need to understand the local regulations for renovations in that region as well as the customs and processes for employing workers. In short, it can become a rather complicated bureaucratic process that is best handled by third party professionals whom you hire, which will require quite a bit of pocket change. The good news is that, just as in your own country, once you find your "in," you are in. However, the cautionary advice being offered here is to ensure that you have plenty of time and funds before you even begin to think nationally or globally. In short, it is usually best to start at home and expand outward.

SCOUTING

When you are out driving neighborhoods, do not only look for houses with For Sale signs in front of them. Look for properties that show signs of being vacant or are unusually unkempt for the area. Look for overgrown grass and landscaping that has not been maintained, notices taped to doors, or boarded windows. Sometimes these properties are prime targets for flipping opportunities. These homes could be involved in estate escrow as the result of a death, going through the foreclosure process, occupied by the very elderly with no relatives nearby, or owned by someone who has encountered financial difficulties and may be motivated to sell. If you find a property that interests you, watch it regularly. If its status does not change or it continues to decline, begin checking city or county records to check the status of the home. Interview neighbors to see if they can give you any further information. This process is called scouting.

Professional scouts are actually considered by many to be a third type of flipper. In this book, however, they are being included in the section on scouting, because I do not consider them flippers in the true sense of the term. A scout is never actually involved in any part of the home buying process. Rather, they are a sort of housing headhunters. Scouts will search for and follow leads for prime flipping properties. They will then sell their information to investors who do buy houses. Some flippers use scouting to get their foot in the door before graduating to full fledged investing and flipping. If you don't have the credit or cash flow to jump directly into flipping, beginning as a scout may be a good way to get into the business and circulate your name while improving your credit and saving money.

How does scouting work? It can actually be as simple or as complicated as the individual acting as a scout chooses to make it. In its simplest form, a scout can simply be the errand person for an investor — someone he or she sends out to search for available properties in a specific neighborhood. This type of scouting may simply involve searching for homes that may be on the open market, but not necessarily advertised in the most lucrative manner, such as homes for which the owners are acting as the agents. Another type of scout acts on his or her own terms and then proactively seeks investors who may benefit from the information gathered. These individuals will locate properties that are in disrepair and appear to be unoccupied and are not currently listed on the market, and they will visit city and county records offices to locate the owners. They may then contact those owners directly to see if they might be motivated sellers. If they are, the scout then has a potentially viable flip for an investor that is not available to the mass market, since the owner is not actively seeking to sell the property.

One word of caution to would-be professional scouts, however, is to remember that a good deal of your integrity will rest on your ability to deliver. Therefore, it is important that you can deliver what you promise. In order to do this, you must be very good at reading people. If an owner agrees that he or she may be interested in selling simply from pressure to do so, that owner may not turn out to be such an avid negotiator. Although the investor to whom you shopped the deal may become frustrated with the owner, he will be equally frustrated with you, because you brought this deal to the table. If you plan to earn a decent income as a scout, then it is important for you to form partnerships with investors, which you do by carrying through on your promised product.

Expect to earn more of a part-time income as a scout when you are first starting out. Since scouts merely sell information and have virtually no involvement in the real estate transactions themselves, they naturally earn the least amount of any of the parties involved. A few hundred dollars for a good lead is typically considered a fair price. One benefit of being a scout, however, is that you are technically a service provider and not a real estate professional, and that means you escape many of the pitfalls of the tricky real estate laws when tax season rolls around.

EVALUATING PROPERTY POTENTIAL

When determining whether a property is a good investment for flipping, it is important to carefully weigh the pros with the cons and to be honest with yourself about the time and budget that will be required to bring the house to retail quality. Aesthetics can usually be repaired in a short time and with a minimal budget. Often times, it is amazing what a simple coat of paint will do. However, some properties require considerably more extensive work. Problems such as termites, foundation cracks or flaws, old roofs, bad plumbing, or outdated electrical wiring can quickly eat your budget and destroy your timeline. If a property will require any of these types of work, it is critical to weigh the costs of having such a large project completed with the other improvements that will also be needed against the potential profit. If the property will require work that will cost more than what you stand to earn, obviously, it is not a good investment. If you are unsure how to determine if a house has these problems, hire an inspector. The fee could be invaluable to you later. If you are feeling the pressure to make a decision immediately, make your offer contingent upon an inspection. This will buy you some time to have the property checked out thoroughly.

Likewise, do not be scared away by sheer ugliness. Even a fair amount of cosmetic cleanup can be done cheaply in contrast to the tens of thousands of dollars it can cost to repair a foundation or rewire an entire house. Often, when appearance is the only aspect of a house that requires improvement, there will be more sweat and elbow grease involved than money.

It is important when viewing a property to keep an eye out for issues that may prove to be costly to fix. Although some of them are most easily found by a professional home inspector, some have telltale signs that are detectable to virtually anyone who is monitoring for them. Take paper and pen with you to take notes as you tour the property.

- **Note the materials out of which the house has been constructed and weigh it against the typical climate of the area.** For instance, in areas near the ocean, the naturally high salt content in the air tends to have an adverse affect on wood. Therefore, it is a good idea to be particularly cautious of wood-sided properties in such a region and to inspect thoroughly the condition of the wood. If it has rained recently, make note of water drainage. If there are multiple puddles in the yard, it could be a sign that there is not proper irrigation for the property. This could have an adverse affect on the conditions of the house.

- **When you enter the house, how does it smell?** A damp or moldy smell could be indicative of poor or no insulation, leakage, mildew, or mold. Although these types of problems are often most obvious in basements, they can sometimes be found throughout the house, particularly in high moisture climates. If the property utilizes a septic system, be on the alert for a gassy or sewage smell. There may be issues with the septic system.

- **Are there hot and cold spots in the house?** While there is an ever-so slight chance that it may mean that you have ghostly visitors, it is most likely a sign that there is either poor circulation or problems with the heating and cooling systems. A simple and inexpensive fix such a cleaning the vents could also be the solution, but it is still important to make note of these types of problems and to determine their cause.

- **How abundant are electric outlets?** In older homes, this is crucial. In today's gadget and electronically oriented society, one outlet in each room is not practical. If there are too few outlets, you are probably going to need to bring an electrician in to install more. While this in and of itself should not make or break your decision to purchase a piece of property, it could also be your first indication that the wiring is outdated and may need replacing, which is a costly venture and something that should definitely be carefully considered before you decide to buy. Also, ask the owners how often they find themselves changing light bulbs. If it is frequently, do some more fishing to find out if it could possibly be attributable to an electrical problem or if they are just in the habit of leaving lights on throughout the house.

- **In the bathrooms and kitchen, check around the toilet and sinks for evidence of leakage.** Water stains or wet spots may be a sign that there are issues with the plumbing. Check faucets and exposed pipes for evidence of rust as well. This could mean corrosion, which may be a sign of larger plumbing issues. Another good sign of plumbing or leakage issues are water spots on ceilings. Be sure to look up as well as around when you are touring a piece of property.

- **Check walls for cracks and plaster breaks.** Simple cracks may be somewhat easy and inexpensive to fix, but it is important to determine first that they are not a sign of larger structural issues. Particularly in older houses in which the walls are made of plaster, large gaping holes are generally not reparable and typically need to be reconstructed, which could get very expensive.

- **In the basement and outside, check for issues with the foundation.** If the house is built on a crawl space, check for problems around the outside of the house. It is also a good idea to consider geological makeup of your area in relation to the type of foundation as well. For instance, in particularly sandy conditions, full basements are not generally a good idea. Even if there are not currently any problems, the tendency of the ground to shift could eventually lead to issues later. In such a climate, a crawl space or cement slab is probably the most desirable foundation.

If you are not accustomed to checking houses for potential red flags, it is a good idea to bring a professional inspector with you, if not to the first walk through, then to any subsequent ones. Typically, a house inspector can be hired for $200-$300, but it can save you up to ten times that in unexpected repairs.

If you can, create a list concerning other features of the house that may not directly figure into your decision to purchase the house, but will eventually be useful information when you are creating your renovation budget.

- **On the list, leave space to record information regarding the age of major appliances, carpet, hot water tanks,**

air conditioning units, and the roof. If the owner is unable to tell you the last time the roof was replaced, for example, that is probably a good indication that it may be time to replace the roof.

- **Also, make sure you record the capacity of the hot water tank and keep this in mind as you tour the house.** Is it sufficient for the number of sinks, showers, and bathtubs in the house?

- **If the house has a fireplace, ask the seller if it is functional and, if so, ask when it was last cleaned.**

- **Make a note of how many outlets, cable, and telephone jacks are in each room.** Also, record any built-in features, such as shelving.

- **Count the number of closets in the house.** Is the storage space in relation to the size of the home adequate, or is that a feature you may consider expanding or adding when you renovate?

- **Note which rooms in the house have built-in light fixtures, as well as what type of natural lighting each receives.** Is it sufficient or does lighting need to be added? If so, it is a good idea to remember that this is a cost that can add up quickly and, although it is not necessary, it is very desirable to many potential buyers and something you may want to consider.

- **Note the countertop materials in bathrooms and kitchens.** Like lighting, this is another feature that many potential buyers scrutinize.

One of the unfortunate aspects of investing is that timing is, more often than not, key, and you are forced to make split second decisions after having only had the opportunity to tour a house once. Many retail buyers often tour a house at least twice before making the final decision to buy. However, in the investment world, competition can sometimes be fierce and in the time it takes to arrange a second tour of a property, it can be sold and the closing paperwork well on the way to being signed. This means that sometimes you are going to have to make decisions based on some rather ambiguous information and without the benefit of all of the details on your list being neat and tidily arranged. As you become more experienced in purchasing real estate, you will learn what is important to look for and how to sum up a property rather quickly. In the interim, it is highly recommended that you arrange to take a house inspector with you when you a tour a home.

Sometimes you may not even have the benefit of being able to tour a property before buying. Many bank-owned properties are like this. When this happens, do what you can to gather as much information as you can about the condition of the home. Ask former owners and bank officials if they can provide this information to you. Although you may not be able to tour the property since such types of property are often sold "As Is," relevant information about the state of disrepair is often made available to anyone who requests it. However, a disclosure is often included excluding the bank (or whoever owns the house) from liability concerning the accuracy of the information.

Once you have evaluated the condition of the property and decide that it would be a good investment, it is time to establish a few facts in order to determine how realistically within reach the home actually is.

1. The first and most logical piece of information you will want to know, if you do not already, is why the owner wants to sell. Is he moving? Are there financial issues? Some answers that are not necessarily deal breakers, but red flags to consider, are comments regarding neighbors or the neighborhood, particularly strict homeowner or historical codes, dissatisfaction with the performance of the school system, and high property taxes. These could all be signs of deeper trouble and, although they may not turn out to be deterrents from purchasing the property, they do warrant some investigation, because they will ultimately affect either your construction and renovation efforts or the decision of potential buyers to purchase the home once you have completed the project. Sometimes this information is established prior to your touring the property. In these instances, it is possible to do any necessary research prior to seeing the property, so that you may view it with a clear and realistic picture of the situation.

2. The second thing you will want to establish is how soon the owner hopes to sell. If they give you an answer that indicates they hoped to sell yesterday, that is a good sign. Chances are, you are dealing with a motivated seller. However, if the response to this question is closer to an answer that indicates that the owner doesn't know or has not really given the issue much thought, this could be an indication that the seller is currently only toying with the idea of selling the property. When this is the answer you receive, follow it up by establishing what the owner hopes to achieve by selling. Does he need money? Has he purchased another home?

3. Finally, you will want to establish how flexible or motivated the seller is. If he seems bent on the asking price, you are going to have a tough time when you enter into negotiations. On the other hand, if the property is in fairly decent shape and the asking price is fair, this is not really much of an obstacle at all, only a formality.

You may occasionally find more than one property in which you would like to invest and will be faced with comparing them in order to choose. Assuming you are working within a target neighborhood, we will not discuss the issue of location, because all potential properties will, theoretically, be equal in that respect. Therefore, the next determinant for you to consider is size. However, when considering square footage, it is important to consider the potential square footage of a piece of property with the current useable space. For instance, if one of the potential properties is a three bedroom house with rather small rooms and a poor layout and the other property is a roomy two bedroom with enough useable space to convert it to three, then it may be the better investment to purchase the two bedroom home and convert it to a three bedroom, rather than simply purchasing the three bedroom home, if you determine that the cost of the conversion is within your budget and will add enough value to justify the alterations. That said, it usually is understood in the world of real estate that if the opportunity presents itself for you to add a bedroom and/or a bathroom, you should do it. A three bedroom home will usually sell for a higher price than a two bedroom home, and a property with two bathrooms will inevitably fetch a higher price than a house with only one.

Assuming both properties are equivalent in size, next consider condition and special features. Perhaps the previous owners of one property recently redid the kitchen, which means that the amount of work and, more importantly, money that you will need to spend on renovating the kitchen will be minimal, whereas, the kitchen in the other house will need to be gutted and reconstructed. When condition is not always such an obvious factor, do a side-by-side comparison of features. Does one house have bigger closets? A working fireplace? Jacuzzi tubs? These are just few of the things that may give one property an edge over another.

When evaluating the actual price and profit potential of a property, there are a few things to consider other than the purchase, renovation, and selling prices. Essentially, any expense you incur in obtaining, refurbishing, and selling the house is an expense which deducts from your profit. This means that things such as underwriting fees, closing costs, holding costs, and maintenance expenses should be figured into your overall equation. Many new investors fail to consider these things and realize only too late that their profit will be considerably smaller than they originally planned.

NEGOTIATING THE DEAL

Once you have found the property you want, you have to secure it. If you are the only potential buyer, this will not be as complicated of a process as it would otherwise be if you had competition, but there are still specific steps that must be taken.

- **Do your math.** Have the figures worked out in your head. Do not just pull a figure out of the air. Before you make an offer, know the typical price range of homes in the retail market in your area, and estimate how much it is going to cost you to bring the house to that condition. Add the purchasing price of the house to the renovation costs and subtract them from the selling price, and that is your profit potential. Use that as a starting point. If you would like a larger profit, bid low and negotiate your way to a happy medium. It is also important to know your bidding ceiling before you start. Know the minimum profit you expect to generate from the sale of the property, and figure the maximum amount you can pay in order to realize realistically that profit.

- **The inspection list you made while touring the house can be used as a great negotiating tool.** If a homeowner is unwilling to come down on the asking price, then use your list to have some of the potential expenses you expected to incur after you bought the property resolved. If the hot water heater needs replacing, for instance, counter the seller's offer with a contingency that you will agree to a higher price if they will replace the hot water heater.

- **Leave room for negotiation, and never make a closed offer.** Always leave yourself room to wheel and deal. When figuring up your numbers, it is usually better to establish a range rather than set numbers. This gives you room to negotiate the best deal and helps the seller feel as though he has options. In the end, it is the best way to achieve a win-win feeling for everyone.

- **Know your facts.** Do not limit your homework to home prices in the area. If you can, find out what position the current owner of the house is in. Why is he selling? Does he have to sell? Is there some sort of financial burden weighing on him that he cannot overcome? Is he in danger of foreclosure? All of these things could have an impact on how you will want to negotiate the deal. Someone who is more or less just tinkering with the idea of selling or who has no reason not to be in a hurry to sell is going to be less willing to give away ground in negotiations than someone who needs money very quickly and is motivated to sell because of it.

- **Establish relationships.** It goes without saying that you should already be friendly with your agent. In this particular situation, your agent as your friend becomes particularly valuable because he can be your voice from a business perspective. If your agent and you have taken the time to get to know each other, your agent will be able to plead more effectively on your behalf to the seller's agent. It is also important to establish a relationship with the seller, if possible. Make yourself stand out among your competition. Treat the seller almost as a client instead of an obstacle standing between you and an object of desire.

- **Do not do third party negotiating.** Simply put, go straight to the source. Find out who will have the final say on the sale of the property, and do everything you can to gain direct exposure to this person. This is often most efficiently accomplished by simply asking the question, "When do you plan to make a decision?" At this point, many sellers will often either state that they must first discuss the matter with their wife, husband, partner, co-owner, etc. If they do not specifically identify the other person(s) involved, they will typically still use the pronoun "we." When they do, simply ask them to identify who else is involved in the "we" to which they are referring. This will help you establish the seller's hierarchy structure and where the individual with whom you are currently speaking falls within it. If your initial contact is hesitant about giving any answers concerning negotiations, chances are that he or she is just an acting agent and has little or no say in the final decision. Upon establishing this, save your negotiation efforts for the time being, because they will be wasted at this stage of the game.

- **Do not allow yourself to form a sentimental attachment to a property.** This is the most common mistake of all potential buyers. Forming an attachment to a particular house will cloud your judgment and may lead to a financial mess, because you will be more likely to be persuaded to stray from your budget or pay more for a piece of property than it is actually worth or, more importantly, more than you will ever be able to get back out of it.

- **Do not make negotiations personal.** This is a business transaction, and you are a business owner. A seller is attempting to get the highest possible price for his or her property, and you are attempting to attain it for the lowest possible price. If both parties are able to remain reasonable and rational, then chances are that you will be able to work out something. However, if either becomes emotional or unreasonable, the best thing may be to walk away from the table. Sometimes, this may mean that the seller will move on to the next potential buyer, who may be swayed into a bad deal more easily than you. If that happens, do not waste time in should-haves and could-haves. Instead, think of the buyer as someone who saved you from a bad deal, and move on to the next property. There are also times when the seller will eventually realize he or she has been unreasonable. If this happens, your professionalism may ultimately pay off for you in the form of the deal you were hoping to get.

Overall, if you give the impression of being a human being attempting find a win-win situation for everyone involved instead of a money hungry investor who will stop at nothing to secure the property, you will be a lot more successful in the end. Remember, unless the seller is in dire financial straits with the bank knocking on the front door while you are knocking on the back, the seller ultimately decides whose offer he accepts. The trick is often times not in the numbers themselves, but in the way in which you present yourself as a person.

Some investors will play a considerably more dangerous game of helping somewhat cunning and stubborn sellers feel as though they are walking away from the table with the better end of the deal. However, I do not particularly recommend this type of negotiation. Although it can work out in the end and be somewhat profitable, you can also end up being burned. My primary argument against this type of bargaining is that, if the seller is willing to deceive in order to sell, then it is worth questioning what other aspects this seller is willing to hide or cover up during the sale. You could be fooled about the status of the property, the condition, or anything in between. Although there are exceptions, my experience has been that conducting an honest business transaction is a two-way street and requires equal integrity from both parties.

AUCTION, BANK OWNED, FORECLOSURE, AND OWNER SELLING PROPERTIES

Acquiring certain properties requires a special and often times specific approach because of the conditions under which they are being sold. Potential foreclosures, bank owned, and auction properties are such types of real estate. In these situations, there are often special processes for acquiring these properties. Potential foreclosures are the most sensitive, because they involve wheeling and dealing directly with homeowners who are often in desperate financial situations. These types of people are often convinced that everyone is out to get them, and the key to negotiating deals with these homeowners is not in the details of the house itself but in convincing them that you are not out to take advantage of them like their creditors and the bank. Bank-owned properties are often obtained directly from the bank, which requires following a detailed procedure established by the bank. The trick to acquiring these types of properties is not in the procedure itself, but in finding an "in" that will allow you to establish yourself with the bank. Auction properties usually involve some type of pre-registration process in order for you to be able to bid on potential properties.

Houses are often auctioned for one of two reasons: they are bank or government-owned, or they are part of a deceased's estate. Bank-owned homes are often foreclosures for which the previous owner stopped making payments, so the bank went through the process of legally exercising their lien on the property. In order to recoup some or all of their lost funds, they will place the house up for auction. A government-seized home, on the other hand, is property the government has seized in connection with some sort of federal crime for which the penalty allows the government to take possession of the offender's property, such as tax evasion or drug trafficking. The government will auction the house in order to be relieved of the burden of maintaining it. Most of the time, auctions are straightforward business. A minimum opening bid is established, and interested buyers will bid against each other until the person willing to pay the most for it is the only remaining bidder. However, some government auctions do have pre-established guidelines detailing who can participate, and in some cases, there is a pre-approval process. It is important to check the stipulations of government auctions before attempting to bid.

Many times, when the owner of the property is the lender, a minimum bid price will be established prior to the auction. This is usually either fair market value of the house or the amount owed on the loan note. In these situations, an auction property is not always a good buy or a bargain. Assuming these types of properties are always a good deal is somewhat akin to assuming that it is always cheaper to purchase food at the local wholesale club. Sometimes, what seems like a real bargain actually translates into a lot of wasted cash and food. In the real estate market, an auction bargain can similarly turn into an expensive waste of money and effort.

Although auction properties are usually not available to tour prior to the sale and are typically sold unseen and "as is," it is important to do some homework in these situations. You should determine the typical selling price of properties in the area to determine if your best buy is from the local wholesale club, or if you would be better off sticking to a good sale in the retail market. Check MLS listings and sale notices to determine what selling prices have been in the neighborhood in which the auction property is located. Compare the conditions of these homes with what you know of the condition of the auction property. Then do your research to determine the general property values of the neighborhood for the past several years. Has it gone up, down, remained steady? This will help you determine a minimum, median, and maximum price range for property in the area. Using this range, you can balance those amounts against the estimated cost of renovations and repairs you anticipate will be required in order to figure out if the lender owned property is a good buy.

Sometimes a homeowner who is in danger of foreclosure will sell in a last ditch effort to avoid the foreclosure. These can be both ideal and somewhat awkward situations. The upside is that you can often get these types of properties at a very good price, since the owner is in somewhat of a desperate situation and attempting to avoid an even more desperate one. However, you may encounter a homeowner who is convinced the whole world is against him as a result of his financial difficulties and is rather hostile toward potential buyers. In these situations, the trick is to convince the homeowner that you would like to help him out in assuming ownership of the house and that you are not an agent of the bank who is attempting to scam him like they did. Present yourself to these types of people as someone who is providing a service. Regardless of whether you initially meet with the open arms of relief or by warring homeowners prepared to do battle with anyone who tries to take their house from them, you will want to confirm just how far into the foreclosure process the home is before you buy. If formal foreclosure has not yet started, then it is safe to proceed. Often times, the foreclosure process can often times be stopped at any point by bringing the payments on the house current. Nevertheless, some lenders have stipulations that create a sort of point of no return. In short, make sure the house can still be legally bought and sold before you enter into an agreement with the current owner.

When a property is particularly tempting and the homeowner is unwilling to negotiate, sometimes it is possible to purchase the loan for a pending foreclosure directly from the lender. Since this process is specific to individual lenders, it is impossible to discuss exact terms here. However, you can generally expect to pay anywhere from 70%-100% of the amount owed on the loan. Some lenders also have a blanket policy in which, by procedure, they give the homeowner a specific amount of time to respond to their foreclosure notice before selling the loan note. Therefore, even though a lender may be interested in selling the loan, you may have to play a waiting game.

In recent years, buying and selling mortgages that are in danger of being foreclosed has become a lucrative, albeit risky, market of its own. Be prepared for competition. The lender wants to recoup what is owed, but is also a business, so if several investors are vying for the same mortgage, note that it is not necessarily going to be first come, first served. It may be an under-the-table auction game in which the highest bidder takes the prize.

If you acquire a mortgage loan that is pending foreclosure, it will be your responsibility to carry out the foreclosure and assume possession of the property. If you do not, and the borrower remains in arrears, it is no longer the lender's money that is being defaulted; it is yours. This means that your income to debt ratio is adversely affected and, if you do not take action, this property could significantly diminish your buying power as well as your ability to purchase other properties, until it is resolved.

Sometimes, homeowners will market their homes themselves simply because they do not want to pay commission fees to a real estate agent. Dealing directly with an owner can be good, because before you even begin negotiations, all of the middlemen have been eliminated. Everything that takes place about the deal will be strictly between the owner and yourself. Unfortunately, this can sometimes be a disadvantage too. Whereas an agent might be able to advise him that it s a good idea to accept your offer contingent upon the inclusion of the kitchen appliances, an owner often has no experience selling homes; therefore, he has difficulty seeing beyond his own, which will make him much less willing to negotiate, particularly concerning any aspects of the house for which he has developed an emotional attachment. Real estate professionals keep the deal an objective business transaction.

The fact that a homeowner is unwilling to pay the fees to a licensed agent could indicate one of two things about him. First, it could indicate that if he was unwilling to pay a 4%-7% fee to an agent, he may not be willing to give much ground in any negotiations. Second, it could indicate that because he is saving 4%-7% of the sale price on real estate fees, he is more willing to compromise a little in the deal. Either way, you will probably be able to get a feel for which one he is after speaking with him for only a short amount of time. If the seller turns out to be the former, sometimes the best approach is to make an offer that you are sure will be one of the higher offers he receives, yet leaves you enough room to generate a profit from the sale of the property. Tell him you would appreciate a call if he changes his mind, and then go home and wait. Once he realizes that his best offer was yours, he will call you, because this type of buyer is motivated by money. Simply put, the highest bid is going to be the one he accepts. If the homeowner is the latter, then use his flexibility to get what you can, but still avoid taking complete advantage of him. Remember, always be professional. The deal in which you take advantage of someone may come back around to haunt you in the form of a black spot on your reputation, which could be considerably more costly to repair than any flip you will ever do.

MAKING AN OFFER

In a more traditional home buying situation, you will make an offer for a property in which you are interested. When making an offer, as in negotiating a deal, it is important to try to understand what it is that the seller wants out of the deal and how that relates to what you need. Determine the ideal and then decide for what you will settle. Then, to the best of your ability, determine your competition. Does there seem to be many interested parties, or did the seller almost emulate desperation? Of course, you will have a little bit more room to make demands in your offers if there are fewer prospective competitors. However, the trick is to present an offer that will not scare the seller away altogether without first presenting a counteroffer, yet still includes your wish list. This can be achieved by presenting an offer that is the right combination of money, assurance, and speed.

While it is true that sometimes the higher the down payment you present the better the chances that the seller will accept your offer, there are other factors that may flip the tables in your favor. If you are ready to move, then offer to close quickly. Some sellers really just want to move on, and if they are forced to wait six more weeks or even two months, that means two more mortgage payments. Therefore, they may be willing to accept an offer of a lower down payment with a speedier closing instead.

Almost all sellers nowadays ask for a letter of financing approval or pre-approval before they will even consider an offer. The reason for this is quite simple. A tremendous amount of time and energy is wasted in the negotiations and acceptance of an offer only to have the buyer's financing fall through. Therefore, it is a good idea to be prepared. Once you have your financing in order or a lender is willing to grant you a mortgage loan, go ahead and obtain a letter of pre-approval that you can present with your offer.

When touring a potential property, always verify what is and what is not included with the house. Never assume. If you ask about something, such as an appliance, that is not initially included but you would like it to be, ask for it in the offer. Many times sellers can be persuaded to include items that they did not initially intend to sell with the house for the right offer. If they do not wish to negotiate the sale of something in the house, they will disclose it in the counteroffer.

Always be sure to leave yourself an out in the form of a contingency to your offer. A contingency allows you to back out of an accepted offer to buy without penalty or further obligation. Make sure these contingencies secure your earnest money. As long as there is a contingency tied to your earnest money, then it is still refundable. However, if you do not include any conditions in your offer that address your earnest money and then you back out of an offer based on one of your conditions, even though perfectly fair and legal, it may cost you the earnest money you included up front.

8

SELL OR HOLD?

T he inevitable struggle for real estate investors is in knowing when to hold a property in order to allow it to appreciate in value, which will ultimately net a higher profit, and when to sell. Several options exist and timing is the key to all of them. When deciding what to do, consider the state of the market. Is it in the midst of a slump? Do you stand to gain more by holding on to the property while weathering the slump or would it be best to do a few minor improvements and turn a quick flip? Is this particular property right for renovation or should you transfer it immediately? Of course, if you have decided to pursue your career in flipping exclusively as either a dealer or a retailer, then these decisions are bit clearer. However, for those who hope to generate earnings utilizing the method of flipping that will earn them the largest profit in a flip, there are many factors to consider.

The condition of the market, your financial well being, and

the actual economy at large can all play a role in the decision to hold on to a property or flip it immediately. Some flippers actually make a career out of simply buying houses and immediately selling them. This type of flipping or dealing, as it is known within the industry, is a profitable niche for those who have neither the desire nor the patience for long term projects and who can overcome the perplexity of the laws governing real estate. Whichever approach an investor chooses, the strategy involved in the decision making process is often as complex as that used to decide whether to buy the property.

Sometimes investors simply become overwhelmed or exhausted by a flip that proves to be a particularly large headache, and they simply wish to unload the property. That is okay, too, and sometimes it is just wise. One of the primary themes of real estate, if you have not already noticed it, is always to leave yourself an out. Never box yourself into something that can lead to the ruin of your business. If a property is just simply not working for you, get rid of it.

IMMEDIATE TRANSFER—THE ART OF BEING A DEALER

If you are the type of person who can see a diamond in the rough but really do not feel like polishing it, the role of dealer might be ideal for you. The trick to being a dealer is being able to seek out properties that are either on the market or whose owners are willing to sell for significantly less than what they are the worth. Remember; a dealer makes his profit from the immediate resale of the property. Therefore, there must be enough room in the deal for you to make a profit in the resale and for the investor who purchases it to make a profit upon resale. The primer types of properties for dealers are those that are in a neighborhood that is on the verge of a rebirth. This will often allow you the opportunity to get more than a good deal on a piece of property that those who only bet on sure things might otherwise see as intimidating. You will still be able to resale at a profit to an investor who has a talent for forecasting to get in on the ground floor with the anticipation of rapid appreciation.

Some question the ethical issues of being a dealer and whether or not it is a form of scamming. The facts of the matter are that supply and demand is at the heart of capitalism. If you have something someone else wants and you can sell it to them at a price that is fair, is reasonable, and is a suitable project to earn them a profit, then you have acted professionally. As long as you disclose all relevant information concerning the property to the investor in your sale and you are not intentionally attempting to artificially inflate the market value of property in the area, then you have not misrepresented yourself in any way. You may have the talent to locate those properties ideal for flipping, but you are not particularly interested in or equipped with the skills to do the work to bring them to retail standards. You, as a businessperson, are still entitled to acquire the property with the intention of finding a suitable investor to realize the full potential of the property. One could even argue that in doing so, you are performing a service of sorts. Earning a profit is what business is all about, so unless one has a wish to argue that trying to make money is wrong in the most generalized form, dealers are not unethical in their nature. As with any business, there are unethical dealers, but the profession itself is not questionable.

In order to maintain ethics, though, it is important to stay abreast of the sometimes-legal parameters of flipping. There are very specific clauses in some contracts and mortgages that apply specifically to double closings, which are the bread and butter of dealers. It is important to follow these legalities, not only for ethical affirmation, but to keep your business and reputation professional and avoid governmental interference. For instance, although you can close with your seller and retailer in the same transaction, it is not advisable. It is perfectly legal. However, seeing you turn from one party immediately to the other may plant the seeds of doubt in both parties' heads, leaving the former to think he could have sold at a higher price and the latter to think he could have bought for less and both thinking you have taken advantage of them. Instead, it is recommended that you do two separate transactions: the first with your seller and the second with your investor. In doing so, not only will everyone feel satisfied, but also you will be drawing a definitive line between the transactions, making them two separate business deals, and that will preserve the ethical stance from a business perspective.

Of course, it is also necessary to give careful consideration to the legal aspects of your deals. Be sure to check with the lender that is providing the financing to confirm that there are no seasoning restrictions. Seasoning restrictions are clauses lenders attach to mortgage contracts to prevent double or simultaneous closings, since many lenders consider this a bit of a risk. Seasoning clauses simply state that a piece of property must be held by a new owner for a certain amount of time before it can be transferred. It is also a good idea to check the specific requirements for deeds in the area in which you are purchasing.

It should be noted that, due to the sensitivity of the situation one faces as a dealer, many dealers are also real estate agents. It is much easier and much less questionable for an agent to conduct a transaction with one party and then, within a couple of hours, conduct a second transaction with another party. The fine line of sensitivity in this approach, though, is that an agent who is not careful can very easily wander into areas that could be classified as conflicts of interest, so it is important that agents consider their approach as a dealer.

REHABBING—FROM WHOLESALE TO RETAIL

Although it obviously comes with fewer questions of its ethical qualities, the field of retail flipping has considerably more dilemmas from an entrepreneurial standpoint. Because it is a significantly larger time commitment, it requires a larger financial commitment. Most retailers err not in their ethical approach, but in their failure to determine how much is enough. Of course, the idea behind retail flipping is to purchase a property, hold it for a very short period of time while renovating it, and then immediately sell it for a profit. However, sometimes, between the time an investor assumes a property and the time he is ready to sell it, circumstances change, creating new decisions. Sometimes, immediately selling a home upon completion of renovations does not make good business sense. When this happens, a retailer is faced with the decision of whether to sell the property at a lower price than he originally intended, maintain the property as a rental for a period of time, or hold it long term in order to earn a larger profit from its sale.

A somewhat new and increasingly popular option many professional flippers are exercising is a professional project planner. Professional project planners are simply individuals who contract their services to oversee and supervise the flip of a home. The concept is somewhat akin to hiring a wedding planner to plan your wedding. These individuals typically have a background in either real estate or design and work with you to bring your budget and aspirations together to help you achieve the profit you hope to achieve. If you plan to flip more than one property at once or begin your real estate career part-time while maintaining your full-time employment, a professional project planner may be ideal for you. Although it is an added expense that will detract from your construction budget, a professional may prove to be worth multiple times his fee in the amount of stress and money he will save you from over budgeted and timeline busting projects. If you have little or no experience in the field of real estate, utilizing the services of a professional on your first couple of projects may also be a good method of training, so that you can get an idea of what improvements sell, how to get them done, and when to do them.

Choose your contractors carefully, and plan for the unexpected. Both of these things can very quickly make your profit disappear if you are not careful. Make sure you select contractors with care, that you are in complete agreement about the expectations, and that everything is in writing. If you need to, pay your lawyer to draw up a contract. If you do not know what you are doing, do not attempt to do it yourself at the risk of it turning out to be a very costly mistake later. Always keep in mind that there are going to be change orders to contracts, as well as some unexpected expenses of which you were not originally aware. Furthermore, make sure you leave room in your budget for such occurrences. Rare will be the project in which you do not encounter at least some unexpected expense.

Visit your project site regularly — daily if you can — to ensure the work is being completed as you agreed and to the appropriate standards. If work is not being done, do not avoid being confrontational. One can confront a contractor who is not fulfilling his obligations in a professional manner, and it is a poor project manager who does not. It is your job to keep this project on task and on budget, which means that sometimes you may have to be the bad guy.

Know how your budget stands. Do not rely on loose figures in your head. Look at your numbers on paper daily. This is the only way to know where you are financially. Be on the lookout for unauthorized or unexpected expenses that creep in without your knowledge or prior consent and act accordingly. If someone made a necessary judgment call, accept it and move on. However, if it appears as though one or more of your contractors has decided to build to his standards instead of yours, it may be time to have a talk with that contractor.

Leave yourself an out in your contracts. This allows you to dismiss contractors who are unable or unwilling to fulfill their obligations to you. It is important to be flexible, but it is equally important to remember that every dollar that you go over your budget is one more dollar shaved off your final number. Keep telling yourself that you are a businessperson now. Flipping is your business, and you must conduct it as such.

Remembering to remain neutral about a project can sometimes be the most challenging aspect to real estate investors, particularly to those who are new to the business. Many first timers become emotionally wrapped up in their projects. Instead of sticking to a strict plan to get the house market ready, they begin to chase after their own personal aspirations for the house. This can be, and is, the downfall of many would-be successful investors. Budgets and timelines are cast aside in the effort to achieve the vision one has for a piece of property.

Unfortunately, knowing when to say when is not restricted to only those flippers who choose to renovate property. Many otherwise stable investors can get so caught up in the idea of a great find that they are unable to recognize the reality of a neighborhood that has taken an unexpected turn for the worse or that riding out a market slump while holding onto a particular piece of property will most likely deplete any profit potential it may hold.

KNOWING WHEN TO MOVE ON

Knowing when to move on can be a heart wrenching decision, especially when it becomes obvious that there is no way to unload a property without a loss. However, understanding that it is wise to cut your losses while they are small is just as much a part of being a smart businessperson as is turning a profit. Although it might be tempting to hold a property with the thought that you may be able to turn it around, it is important to remember that with each passing day, you are also spending more money. Three situations, in particular, can often reduce an investor's profit before he even realizes what has happened.

- **Over Improving:** It is oh-so-easy to become so personally wrapped up in a property that you become somewhat obsessed with making it perfect. However, remember that the goal of flipping is to improve a house to the point that it will turn your desired profit. This may or may not mean installing top of the line appliances, replacing the roof and siding, installing hardwood floors, etc. What this does mean is it is essential that, when you do acquire a new property with the intent to rehab, you evaluate it in comparison to other properties in the neighborhood to determine what it will take to make that house comparable to others in the area. Then, set your renovation goals and budget. If you set out to make a perfect house that will ultimately cost you more than you will reap in earnings from the sell of it, you are defeated before you even begin.

- **Market Slumps:** Market slumps are touchy, because sometimes they can be realistically weathered, and it is a good business decision to ride them out. However, sometimes they extend beyond their anticipated duration and can become very costly to investors. When you encounter a market slump as an investor, be honest with yourself about the outlook on the economy in comparison to your budget. If you have the budget, it may be wise to hold a piece of property until the market improves. If the slump is brief and the anticipated profit for a particular property high, it is possible to earn a smaller profit or at least break even in holding the property through the worst part of the slump. However, if the economy appears to be in an extended period of decline and the anticipated profit for the property is not that high, the smartest business decision may be to cut your losses on that particular property and move on before it begins eating your earnings from other properties as well.

- **Bad Investments:** Sometimes problems in properties do not become evident until after the renovation process has begun. Although the improvement budget should be large enough to allow for some of these instances, there are times when the problem is simply too large to compensate for and the best solution is to just resale the property to someone who is willing to spend the money to correct the problem. Again, it is best to be honest with yourself about whether or not pushing on with a sure fire budget-buster in the pursuit of what, in the end, will be a phantom profit eaten away in the renovation, or if it is best to resale early in order to recoup and move on before the project turns into a virtual money pit that pulls all of your finances and literally drives you to financial ruin.

- **Failing to recognize that a piece of property is not going to realize the profit for which you originally planned or hoped:** Although many investors will advise you to hold out for your desired asking price, this is usually neither wise nor profitable in the end. The more unrealistic of a price tag you attach to a piece of property and the less negotiating room you leave potential buyers usually translate to a longer, sometimes indefinite, holding period for you. For each month you own the house, you must pay the mortgage. If the property stays on the market for several months, you will also eventually have to begin investing in the upkeep. In other words, for each month that you own the house, your profit becomes smaller. Remember that asking prices should be aggressive, not unrealistic. Setting a profit range is usually a good way to remedy the ideal of a specific number. Understand the comparable range in the area of a property you undertake prior to assuming the project. It is usually an expensive mistake to attempt to compensate for an over blown budget by inflating the asking price for the property and hoping for the best.

9

RENOVATING PROPERTIES

I n this chapter, we will specifically discuss those issues faced by retail flippers in the renovation process. Once you find and acquire a piece of property ripe for renovation, there will be many decisions to make. What will the budget be? What needs to be done? How long will it take? Should I do the work myself or hire a contractor? Since time is money in real estate, these are all decisions that must be made within a very brief amount of time. Therefore, it is critical to consider several factors when entering into a renovation project.

DETERMINE A BUDGET

Determining a budget can be daunting, particularly if you have never undertaken a large renovation project before. The first thing to do is assess the property. What work will you need to do in order to get the property to the point at which it is likely to sell for the desired asking price? Next, prioritize. Take a piece of paper and divide it into three columns labeled A, B, and C. Then, determine the big projects that *must* be done. These go into the A column. In the B column, list the smaller projects that *should* be done, but do not, in any way, contribute to the home's state of disrepair. Finally, list those improvements you would *like* to make but are neither necessary nor essential to the project in the C column. Congratulations! You have just prioritized your renovations and created an outline for a checklist.

After prioritizing, determine if any or all of the work in your A column will require a contractor or if you can complete the work yourself within your established budget and timeline. Be honest with yourself. It is very easy, at this stage, to fool yourself into thinking you are Bob Vila's equal in any task when in reality, you are more like Tim Taylor. If you have never even picked up a hammer before, it is probably not a good decision to attempt to install drywall yourself. Once you have determined which work, if any, will require a contractor, begin your search for professionals to perform that work. If you have determined that you and your talents are up to the challenge of the DIY approach for any of the work in your A column, begin browsing local home improvement stores at this time, as well, to get an idea of what supplies you will need and what they will cost you. Get price quote printouts, if you can. Once you have interviewed contractors and determined the costs of DIY projects on your A list, it is time to move on to your B list with the remaining budget.

Many new or first time investors have a proper budget but are unsure about exactly on what improvements their dollars are most well spent. To a certain extent, this is largely going to depend on the condition of various aspects of the property when you bought it.

"A" PRIORITIES

Assuming the property is structurally sound, you will want to consider the roof. A roof is a somewhat inconspicuous and is easily forgotten in many rehabbing projects. However, the condition of the roof is not just cosmetic, it is important to the function of the structure. A poorly repaired or rotted roof could affect the efficiency of the heating and cooling systems in the home, as well as be the direct cause of leakage or water damage. Sometimes a roof will simply need to be repaired and may essentially amount to replacing a few shingles. However, sometimes the problem is not the shingles at all, but the wood underneath. If this is the case, the entire roof will need to be replaced. When replacing single shingles, it is also important to remember that most regions have laws concerning the maximum number of shingle layers there may be on a single roof in order for it to pass inspection. Be sure to check your local codes concerning these guidelines.

After the roof, it is important to consider the hot water heater and the heating and air conditioning units. How old are they? According to industry experts, the average life of a hot water heater is 8-12 years. For an air conditioning unit, it is 12-16 years, depending on whether it is a 10 or 12 SEER model. Heating units should be replaced approximately every 14 years. If any of these units are within two years of their average life expectancy and are showing signs of their age, it would be a good idea to figure them into your budget.

Next, look at the gutters and downspouts. Even if they need to be replaced, this can be done inexpensively. More often than not, however, they merely need to be cleaned. Although cleaning gutters is a DIY project that can be done for very little money, it involves a lot of grunt work, so if you are not the type who enjoys being up to your elbows in dirt and grime, you might want to consider budgeting for a professional to do this job, which can be done somewhat affordably.

Consider plumbing and electrical issues. Is there a shortage of outlets? Is there any lighting in the house that does not work, even when the bulbs have been changed? Are there any exposed wires or burn lines on the walls? Any of these may be an indication that you will want to elevate lighting to an "A" level project on your list. When evaluating the condition of the electricity, look at the fuse box. Fuses can be purchased by the box at the local home improvement store and are relatively easy to replace, but they are still an important detail that is often overlooked. When considering the condition of the plumbing, check for leaks around faucets, toilets, bathtubs, and showers. These might not necessarily be indications of a large problem, but you will still want to resolve them. A leaky faucet, for instance, may simply need a washer replaced. This can be done in a matter of minutes from a kit that can be picked up from your local home improvement store for a nominal amount of money. Sometimes small leaks around toilets, showers, and bathtubs can be resolved with re-caulking. However, if a small lake forms every time the toilet is flushed or the shower is turned on, it probably means there is a much bigger issue that needs attention. Likewise, look at the exposed pipes. If there is a lot of rust, that could mean that the plumbing is outdated and needs replaced altogether. This can be rather expensive and somewhat time consuming. It is also a good idea to determine the source of any water stains on the ceiling. Are they the remnants of a previous problem that has long since been fixed, or are they a clue to a much larger problem? Whether they are large or small, it is important to address electrical and plumbing issues properly. Even a small leak around a sink may shake a buyer's confidence by thinking that great paint and floors are only a cover up for shoddy craftsmanship underneath.

Next, take a close look at the floors. Aside from outdated, worn, or stained carpet, be on the look out for warped floorboards or cracked tile. When you are considering pulling up carpet to refinish hardwood floors, be sure to evaluate the condition of the floors to determine if they are in a suitable condition to sand, buff, and re-stain or if it would be better to replace them completely. In rooms in which you plan to replace carpet, take stock of the condition of the sub-flooring. Does it need to be replaced as well? In the instance of damaged tiles, be careful when you contemplate replacing just one tile, particularly if the existing tile is rather old. Even though you may be able to match color and design, the natural aging of the old tile may cause your new tiles to stand out like sore thumbs. If there are areas in which you are considering swapping carpet for hardwood or linoleum for tile, if the condition of the existing flooring is otherwise okay but you are unsure your budget will support the change, put those decisions on hold until you have evaluated the remainder of those issues which are crucial and should be made "A" priorities in your project. One exception to this is carpet that is found in either the kitchen and/or bathrooms. Even if this carpet is in good condition, the vast majority of homebuyers prefer some type of non-carpeted surface in these areas, so these areas should be placed on the "A" list, regardless of the condition of the carpeting.

Now, venture back outside and look at the exterior of the home. If it is natural brick or stone, chances are you have gotten very lucky and will not need to refinish the exterior of the home. Sometimes, small issues, such as cracked or missing bricks, will require that a small number of bricks be replaced. The problem is that, like clothing designs, certain styles of bricks are sometimes discontinued. We encountered this problem when we built an addition on to our thirty-year-old home. Finding a close facsimile proved to be somewhat of a chore and when we did find a design close enough to our original to use, when the addition was first completed, there were some obvious differences in aging. It took a couple of years for the new bricks to catch up to the old in appearance, which may prove to be an issue to potential homebuyers who will be seeing the freshly finished product. If the exterior of the home is wood siding, what is the condition of the paint? If it is chipping or bubbling, it is probably time to replace it. If the house is constructed of vinyl siding, you will probably need to replace the siding rather than paint. This could be either good or bad. The good news is that if just a patch of siding needs replaced, this is a lot less expensive than having to replace the siding on the entire house. However, some issues you may run into with this, particularly in older houses, is that the specific color of siding that was used on your property is no longer manufactured or, if it is, it will not be an exact match once it is installed next to the existing weathered siding. Color is also important. Although some would classify this as purely cosmetic, the fact of the matter is that curb appeal is a very important factor to those searching for a home. The bottom line is that if the outside is just not that appealing, it is probably a good idea to rethink the exterior.

Also, consider the driveway. If it is concrete, are there cracks or holes in it? If there are, you should consider having a new one poured. If there are significant cracks in the existing driveway, consider the layout. Some driveways crack because they are laid out in a way for which the ground has not been sufficiently structured to support the concrete. Making a slight shift or ensuring that the new concrete contractor properly prepares the ground will insure that the new driveway stays intact. If the existing driveway is stones or pebbles, have it paved. Not only do buyers prefer finished driveways, but the paving also adds to the curb appeal of the home by giving it a more finished appearance.

The entrance leading to the front door is also important. If it is a sidewalk, are there cracks? If there are, you may want to consider having it repoured as well. If it is stone, check to make sure that there are no missing pieces and that the spacing is sufficient not to feel awkward.

Look at the windows from both the inside and out. How long has it been since they have been replaced? It is recommended that windows be replaced about every twenty-five years. That means that if the property is forty years old and the windows have never been replaced, you should figure the cost of new windows into the project. Although many will argue that this is not necessary if the current windows are in good condition, not replacing windows can lead to the overworking of your heating and air conditioning units, which means an escalated electric bill. Though you may be able to slip this detail by at least half of potential buyers, those doing their homework will inquire about the average monthly cost of electric and heating for the property. If the number you give is significantly higher than comparable homes in the area, inquisitive buyers will immediately sense an underlying issue. They may not immediately make the connection to old windows, but they will be able to figure out that resolving the problem is probably going to cost them a significant amount of money.

If the glass in the window is broken, the entire window most likely will not need to be replaced, only the glass pane. This can be done relatively quickly and inexpensively. Windows and doors also need to be lubricated about once a year, so even if the windows and doors of the property are in good condition, figure the time and costs of lubricating them into your budget. This is going to be a rather nominal cost equal to that of a few cans of WD-40.

Now explore the lot. Are there any major problems that must be fixed? Does the house need landscaping? Does the back yard resemble a prairie reserve? Is the fencing falling down or missing sections? If so, you should plan to correct these problems. Although it is not mandatory that the landscaping of a home look like a cover photo from a home and garden magazine, it is a crucial selling point. Many neighborhoods actually have specific bi-laws concerning landscaping, so be sure to check them for the one in which the property is located. Some guidelines simply required the perimeter of the home be landscaped while others actually specify specific materials that may be used. To develop an educated estimation of the level of strictness in your area without going to check records, simply take a drive around and pay close attention to the landscaping. If all of the designs and flowers are similar, chances are, your newly acquired property is in a neighborhood with restrictive guidelines. However, if the landscaping is pure luck and runs from one end of the gamut to the other, there probably are not many, if any, rules governing the area and, if there are, they probably are not being enforced. Landscaping restrictions tend to be most common in either planned or historic communities, as well, which is another good rule of thumb to consider when making the determination.

Back inside the house, evaluate the appliances. Harvest gold, burnt umber, and avocado green pretty much went out of fashion when the seventies ended, so if the appliances in your newly acquired property are any of those colors, you should definitely plan to replace them. For those homes that have either been built or undergone some type of kitchen renovation since the 1980s, however, the decision may be a bit more difficult to call. The average life of most kitchen appliances is actually 14-16 years. So, start by establishing how long it has been since the appliances have been replaced. Age alone could be your deciding factor here. Remember, "A" list priorities are those things which have to be done, not that you would like to do. Although stainless still is somewhat en vogue right now, it is important to determine whether the budget will support stainless steel appliances in relation to other improvements that must be made before you decide to gut the kitchen. Also, look at the countertops. If they are designed to match the harvest gold, burnt umber or avocado green appliances, you will probably need to replace those too. Likewise, if they are old and significantly scratched and dented, it is probably time for new countertops. The kitchen cabinets are also an important consideration. If they are in relatively good condition, then even if they are ugly, you may not have to replace them. Sometimes painting or sanding down and re-staining old cabinets and replacing the old hardware with new are sufficient updating for sturdy cabinetry. If you would like to replace the cabinets but are not yet sure if your budget will support completely replacing them, put them on your "B" wish list and finish evaluating your "A" list priorities before making a final determination. If your budget will not support completely changing them, it may be possible for you to reface the existing ones. This is a cheaper option that may be a good compromise.

When you finish evaluating the kitchen, move on to the bathrooms. What are the conditions of the tubs and showers? Do they need to be completely replaced, or would a good scrubbing restore them to like new condition? Are they cracked or chipped? If so, you may want to go ahead and plan to replace them, unless they are older pieces, such as claw foot tubs that add architectural interest to the house. In those situations, you may to consider having the tub restored instead of replacing it. Are the toilets stained and worn? If so, it may be time to replace them too. As with the kitchen, if the bathroom cabinetry and countertops are in bad condition, it may be time to change them out as well. However, if they are just ugly, determine how much of your budget will remain after your "A" priorities are resolved before conclusively deciding to change them out. If your funds do not support new ones, it may be time for some creative cosmetic fixes.

After you have determined your "A" priorities, consider the portion of your budget that will be needed for them. In some cases, you may get very lucky, and it will be a very small percent. Other times, almost your entire budget may be eaten by these essential projects. Most of the time, however, there will be money left to move to your "B" list. Your "B" list, as you will remember, are those improvements you would like to make and that will improve the value of the property, but are not threatening the safety or sturdiness of the home in any way. Unfortunately, many flippers, even those who are considerably experienced, fail to distinguish between crucial repairs and those things they would like to do, but are not essential. This mistake is where budgets and timelines go awry. The problem is that it becomes very easy to justify a blow to your budget by telling yourself that it is improving the value of the property. However, it is important to remember that profit was a big factor in determining your budget. Although busting your budget may be adding value to the home, you should be aware that you would eventually, if not immediately, venture into a danger zone from which it will be impossible to recover the total amount of your investment in the sale of the house.

When making your final determinations concerning your "A" priorities, remember to consider aspects that will have an affect on you budget over and above the costs of these repairs themselves. For most plumbing and electrical work, for instance, you are going to have to hire a professional to do the work. Most inspection criteria specifies that installing new wiring or laying new plumbing must be done by someone who is certified in these professions. This is because this type of work must meet certain codes before passing inspection and, in the case of electrical wiring, could be very hazardous to anyone who does not know what he or she is doing. Some regions also require certain work to be completed using specific materials. A professional in your area will already be familiar with these specifications, whereas the typical Do It Yourself guru may not. You will also need to consider things such as permit fees. These are typically not budget breakers but several of them can add up quickly, so it is important to consider their costs. Many areas also have noise or construction ordinances that will prevent work from being done on your property between certain hours or on certain days. This is slightly more important when considering your timeline, but it is still important to your budget. You do not want to have to pay a crew extra money to sit around because you scheduled them to show up at the site to install siding early on a Saturday morning and, when they arrived and began work, a city official was promptly dispatched to inform you that construction is not permitted in your area until after noon on Saturdays.

"B" PRIORITIES

Renovating a house is somewhat like shopping for clothes. Of course, we would all love to stock our closets full of designer labels, but the reality is often that money matters force us to prioritize and purchase at least some of our clothing in much lesser known brands and off the sale rack. The good news about this is that, just as shopping for your wardrobe, this is the part of your project where you get to determine how you want to spend your money. The bad news is that, unlike shopping for clothes, renovating a home is a little less personal, so it is still important to keep buyers in mind when making your choices.

In determining your "B" list priorities, start in the kitchen. This is the one room of the house in which potential buyers will be the most critical, so it is important to be as detailed as your budget will allow. Begin with the appliances. Black, white, or stainless steel are the trends of the day. Stainless steel is the most costly of the three. However, there are different levels of stainless steel appliances as well, so do not automatically assume that option is out before doing a little bit of shopping around. Check unlikely places like local wholesale clubs or local vendors who have a publicly accessible overstock store or section of their warehouse. Sometimes fairly decent deals can be found here. Black and white appliances can be found ranging in everything from budget to high-end price ranges, so if a little bit of browsing convinces you that stainless steel appliances are not in the budget for this project, determine whether black or white would best fit the overall look you are attempting to achieve in the kitchen and start shopping.

Now, review your ideas about the cabinets. How did you feel about them on your first evaluation? If you are happy with them as they are or feel a coat of paint would make them as appealing as replacing them would, then go ahead and save yourself a few thousand dollars by keeping them. If they look like a throw back from the sitcoms you watched as a child, though, it might be a good idea to follow your inclination to change them. One option you might consider, if your budget supports making some improvements to them but not completely replacing them, is refacing. Refacing is simply changing out the fronts of the existing cabinets and is between half and two thirds of the cost of completely replacing the cabinets.

The "B" list phase is the time to review your original ideas about the countertops as well. Granite is the current trend and the most expensive. Corian is also popular and less expensive.

Last but certainly not least on the list of kitchen considerations are the flooring and lighting. Tile and Pergo are most suitable for kitchens. However, when using tile, avoid types that are easily breakable and subject to cracking in temperature changes. Likewise, hardwood is a very common flooring option throughout entire houses, but it is not recommended for the kitchen. The kitchen is usually a high traffic area, so it is important to make sure that the flooring is durable and easy to clean. Hardwood does not stand up well to heavy foot traffic and tends to bubble or warp when it gets wet. Laminate flooring is a good alternative if you want to achieve the look of hardwood with a durable material.

Kitchens should also have plenty of lighting, so make sure things are bright. Small details, such as under-cabinet lighting, can be done inexpensively and go over well with potential buyers. Make sure the kitchen is well lit, but soft. Avoid fluorescents. Lighting that is too stark and powerful will make the kitchen seem more like an institutional facility and less like a comfortable room in the home. Buyers tend to look for kitchens that are warm and inviting, so consider your lighting when making your choice for the paint color.

Finally, do a walkthrough of the kitchen to determine if anything about the layout could be changed in order to make it more user-friendly. Are the major appliances in the right places in relation to each other? Is there a natural flow to the way in which the cabinets are arranged? If anything about the setup is awkward, now is the time to budget that change. Although it is not necessary to go to extremes in renovating the kitchen, between a third and half of your remaining budget after your "A" priorities have been determined should be used to make the kitchen as spectacular as you possibly can.

After you assess the kitchen to determine the "B" priorities that you would like to make a reality during improvements, it is time to move on to the bathrooms. Kitchens and bathrooms can, and often do, sell houses. Therefore, it is important to consider these two rooms. If there is more than one bathroom in the house, start with the master bathroom. If there is no master bathroom, start rethinking the floor plan to determine if there is any way that you can steal some space to create one by either repurposing another room, knocking out a closet or pantry wall, or reclaiming space within the master bedroom. Most contemporary homebuyers strongly prefer a master bedroom with a private bathroom and will often pass over homes they otherwise love in order to have one. If the master bathroom in the home has the space or if you can make it, large soaking tubs, garden tubs, and spa tubs are very popular. Separate tubs and showers are also popular, although often not essential.

If the cabinets are old and outdated, now might be a good time to replace them. In today's market, a couple of options exist to make this renovation more budget-friendly. A current trend is using stand-alone furniture pieces. Capitalizing on this trend allows you to shop around for a piece of inexpensive furniture to place in your bathroom while still making a very fashionable addition to the bathroom. The second option, if your kitchen cabinets are somewhat neutral, is to slip some extra cabinet units into your kitchen order and place them in the bathroom. Not only can this option save you a bit of money, but also it provides uniformity to the look of the house that many people find appealing. Most people prefer double sinks in their master bathroom, as well, so if the current fixture has only one sink, you may want to consider replacing it with one that has two.

Flooring is very important. Carpet is a no-no. Tile is extremely popular. Laminate is less popular but a viable option. One material you should never consider installing in a bathroom, however, is hardwood. It will never be able to withstand the moisture. If the existing flooring is tiled and you plan to keep it, check the grout over. You may need to be regrout, which is actually relatively simple and a lot less expensive than completely retiling the floor.

Lighting should also be adequate. Most people prepare themselves to greet the world in their bathrooms, which means that the lighting should be bright enough to show the imperfections in a person's complexion when she first looks into the mirror in the morning, but soft enough for them not to show when makeup is appropriately applied.

After the kitchen and bathroom, you may want to consider the existing storage space in the house. Are there adequate closets? Could the house benefit from a bit of space re-appropriation in order to create a couple more? Storage space is key to most homebuyers today, and the lack of it can be a deal breaker.

Next, consider replacing things that are outdated, such as wood paneling and carpet. Some other details that are often overlooked but can significantly improve the appearance of a home are hardware, light fixtures, ceiling fans, and light switches. All of these can be replaced rather inexpensively, and they can instantly give an updated appearance to an older home.

Flooring often makes the top of many renovation wish lists. Although there is no dominate preference among homebuyers, some will prefer carpet, while others hardwood, it is worth noting that solid flooring surfaces such as hardwood and laminate are more neutral, allergy friendly, and stronger than carpet. Although it is more expensive to install hard surface flooring, it is usually a better long-term bargain for the buck. On average, carpet will need to be replaced approximately every five years in high traffic areas of the house. However, hardwood and laminate flooring will easily last for three to four times that long. Pergo flooring is practically indestructible. A good way to please most homebuyers and still rein in the budget is to install hard surface flooring in the common areas and carpet in bedrooms. Since there is generally a lot less foot traffic in the bedrooms, carpet will endure longer there than in heavily treaded rooms. Because you split the house between a hard surface and carpet, if potential buyers prefer one or the other, they will be able to make the conversion a lot less expensively than having to do the entire house, which will be a lot less overwhelming, both financially and mentally, to them as they are touring and considering the home.

For existing walls, paint will often do wonders. Although most home interior decorating professionals will tell you that priming is necessary, it is actually only necessary when you are repainting dark walls. For instance, if you want to change the wall color of a room that is currently red to yellow, then you will need to prime the walls. Otherwise, it will take several coats of yellow paint before the red will cease to bleed through, and even then the color might be somewhat diluted. However, if you are changing a wall from a beige or tan color to yellow, primer is not necessary. You will probably have to paint two coats, but any dilution that may have resulted in the coloring will be eliminated in the second coat of paint. In addition to paint, adding molding to a room is another inexpensive way of instantly improving its appearance. Although cutting the edges of the pieces so that they properly fit together is a skill that is acquired through a bit of practice, molding is feasibly a DIY project, if your budget is starting to get a bit tight.

Outside, consider the approach to the house. For instance, if the house is on a hill, are there steps leading to the front door or will visitors be forced to approach the house by walking up the driveway? If this is the case, you may want to consider adding steps leading to the front door. They will make the house seem more welcoming and add curb appeal.

"C" PRIORITIES

In a perfect investment world, after you decide on all of your "A" and "B" priorities, there would be enough room in your budget for "C" priorities. "C" priorities are those projects that investors would like to do, but are in no way detrimental to the value of the home if they are not done. Although these types of projects will often add to the value of the house, they are seldom supported in the renovation budget of someone who flips houses for a living and are not typically standard features in other homes in the area. Often, they are improvements that homeowners can and will do when their budget and needs accommodate them. Simply put, they are features that are nice to have, but are not necessary. However, some examples are being included here, so that if you are ever blessed with unlimited resources, you may consider doing them as part of your project.

Once again, though, I want to caution you again against that danger zone of investing more into the house than what you can realistically expect to get back out of it. Always keep in mind that a $300,000 home will almost never sell for $300,000 in a neighborhood in which the average-selling price is $150,000-$200,000. Most buyers who are interested in a $300,000 home are going to prefer to purchase in an area in which the general flavor and character of the neighborhood reflects that higher standard. As the cliché states, most retail home shoppers would prefer the worst house in the best neighborhood over the best house in the worst neighborhood. So do not just assume that because you put $50,000 more work into a project and theoretically improved the value of the home by $100,000 that you will get that out of it, if that investment makes the final price of the out of line with the general price range of houses in the area.

Some outside improvements that may be attractive amenities include decks and patios. Although decks can be a DIY project, they often require more time and money that your project budget can handle. Since a deck is a feature that many homeowners would like, but is not typically a part of all houses, this is a "C" priority.

Finished attics and basements are another great example of "C" priorities. The extra finished living space is a great feature that can add considerably to the value of a house. Nevertheless, it is often a luxury, not a requirement. The exception to this rule may be when you are working on a particularly small house, and refinishing an attic or basement space could mean adding an extra bedroom. In that instance, you will have a very good chance at recouping your money and this typically "C" level project would be more of a "B" level one. Keep in mind, though, that many zoning codes will require a basement to have a separate accessible entrance before the space can legally be added as living space to the total square footage. Many homeowners bypass this because the door is not a legal requirement. If you plan to advertise the space as part of the total square footage of the home or if you plan to market the space to homeowners, you may need to add one. Depending on the layout and positioning of the house, adding an entrance can be almost as expensive as finishing the basement space. However, if you simply think that finishing the basement would be great because the addition of a game room, exercise room, and wet bar would be great, you should reconsider. Although you are probably right and those features would be great additions to the house, adding them may end up costing you more than the value you will be adding.

Swimming pools, basketball courts, and tennis courts are also all "C" priorities. Not only are these unnecessary expenses to your budget, but they can actually detract from it, because while they will appeal to some potential buyers, they will be considered liabilities by others, which means you can considerably limit your potential buyer market by adding any of these features. If a property already has a pool or a tennis court when you purchase it, however, and it is in decent shape, it is acceptable, not to mention usually the most economical route, to clean and refinish it. However, they typically should not be added to a property, if they are not already there.

Fencing often straddles the various priority lists. In most places, it is a "C" priority list. It is nice to have, but not necessary and is something that the future owners of the house could add if they do feel that it is needed. However, in a handful of places, some sort of fencing is required, in which case it jumps from a "C" to an "A" priority. In my neighborhood, for example, not only is fencing required, there are stipulations regarding the type of fencing that can be erected and the height that it should be. It is a good idea to either ask about or check for these stipulations before you buy a property, particularly if you happen to notice that every single house in the neighborhood has a fenced in yard. Sometimes, too, you may purchase a home in a neighborhood particularly known for its family friendly atmosphere. In this case, a fence may be a "B" priority. It is not required, but it will definitely appeal to parents with children.

Once you have determined your priorities and the effect they will have on your budget, you will have a clearer picture of what work you will be able to realistically do yourself and what projects you will need to seek the services of a contractor to complete.

CONTRACTOR VERSUS DIY

In the excitement of earning a large profit, it is easy to think of yourself as a DIY guru. The harsh reality is that sometimes it turns out to be well worth the money spent on a contractor in the long run. When evaluating the work your property needs to have done, be honest with yourself about your budget, timeline, and the time you have to commit to the project. If you have two days in your timeline to install new kitchen cabinets and you have never installed them before, it is a good idea to consider whether hiring someone to install the cabinets for you and complete within your timeline will ultimately be less costly than the damage you will cause to your budget through the disruption of your timeline. It is also important to check with your local officials to determine if the services of a professional are required in order for certain work to pass inspection. We once built an addition on to our house, for example, which required some new electrical wiring. One of the mandates for new wiring to pass inspection in our area, however, stipulated that all new electrical wiring must be done by a licensed electrician. In this case, DIY was not even an option. Checking for these types of regulations rather than making assumptions can save you a lot of money by avoiding the costly mistake of paying once to do the work yourself and then again to bring in a professional.

Another aspect of hiring a contractor that you may want to consider is the commitment a contractor can make to you.

When interviewing potential contractors, ask them how many other jobs they will be doing while working on your project. If they clearly have a full plate, then no matter how good their reputation is, you may want to look elsewhere for a contractor who is not over committed. Contractors who take on more than they can handle can extend your timeline way beyond what you originally projected and end up costing you a lot of extra money in the end.

Before you even begin to interview contractors, you must have some idea of how much you should expect to pay for services. It is not wise to assume that contractors are quoting a fair price to you. It is also important to appear at least somewhat knowledgeable when speaking with prospective contractors about a job. Although not everyone will take advantage of you, dishonest ones will begin to build up services and fees when they detect that you are completely unfamiliar with the work that must be done. In the end, you end up paying, quite literally, for your lack of knowledge. However, this does not mean that you must take a crash course on becoming a home improvement expert. Start by browsing your local home improvement stores. Without even speaking to anyone, you will be able to form a good idea of what you can expect to pay for parts and supplies. Many of these stores also offer free instruction in a class setting for such projects as installing ceiling fans, laying floors, and painting, if you have the time to invest. Visit your local library or bookstore and peruse books on the subject. It is not necessary to read them cover to cover, but browse through them and read sections that specifically apply to work you will need to have done. Explore the topic on the Internet. Countless Web sites and forums are available on the Internet that will give you a good idea of what you can anticipate your costs to be. Friends or family members who have had similar projects done to their homes are also a good source of information. Once you have done a bit of homework and acquired to have enough knowledge about what you should expect, then you will be ready to interview prospective contractors. In general, you can expect $1 in material cost with $1 in labor costs. This is a conservative estimate but, again, over budgeting and discovering that you will have a little left to do an extra project is better than discovering that you have run out of money with a project still left untouched.

Determining what type of contractor to hire for a job can sometimes be half the battle. If most of your work is going to be professionally done, you may want to consider hiring a general contractor. This will save you a lot of time and headaches because a general contractor assumes the responsibility of organizing and overseeing the general project and often subcontracts all of the side work for you. Hiring a general contractor for a construction project is somewhat on par with hiring a bridal consultant to assist with your wedding. It is still your show and you still are in charge, but you have someone to guide you by telling you what you need to do next, where you need to go to do it, and to be your representative in the negotiations.

If you are a DIY fanatic and intend to do most of the work yourself, then a general contractor may not be necessary, but you will still have to arrange for professionals to complete that work which even the best home rehabbers should not attempt on their own for either safety or regulatory reasons, such as electrical issues. This means that you are going to have to hone those project management and organizational skills. A common trap for many DIYers is that they believe because they are capable of doing the work, then they will have no problem flipping a house. Although being able to do many home renovation projects yourself will come in handy, it will not help you properly schedule and plan. That administrative work requires a very businesslike and less hands-on approach. Before you even pick up a hammer, you are going to need to know what you are going to be doing, how long it is going to take you, and how it relates to the work that will need to be completed by professionals. Then, you will need to schedule those individuals. This also means that you are going to have to stay on task as well.

If you plan to do any work yourself, there are certain tools and supplies in which it would be wise to invest and have on hand for your projects. Although you can rent equipment, repeated rentals can become expensive, and tools will pay for themselves when you consider the price of multiple renters. Begin with a basic toolbox:

- **A 16 oz. all-purpose hammer.** There are many different types of hammers of varying weights and hammers. A 16 oz. hammer is good middleweight and size and can successfully be used for many different tasks. However, if you determine after getting started that you will be doing a lot of construction work yourself, you may want to consider adding other hammers, such as those used for cabinetry or framing, to your collection.

- **A tape measure that measures at least twenty-five feet.** Although the width of the buckle is relatively unimportant, it is a good idea to keep in mind that wider buckles will allow you measure longer lengths without buckling.

- **A level.** A level is a must, particularly when doing projects in older homes that have settled and, therefore, are more likely to have uneven floors or walls. At minimum, your level should be a three-foot level.

- **A miter box and backsaw.** A miter box is the device used to cut trims and crown molding. Even though installing molding is an inexpensive and relatively easy task for most DIYers to master, a miter box makes it even more efficient and relatively full proof.

- **A chalk box.** For all of you weekend warrior rookies, a chalk box is that infamous blue line tool in which you stretch the string to make a line and then snap it. The impression of a blue chalk line is left behind. Quite simply, this tool keeps lines straight.

- **A handsaw.** Although electronic saws have made handsaws almost obsolete, these handy tools still come in handy when you need to maximize your control over the cut being made.

- **WD-40.** A few squirts of this handy product will make even the squeakiest doors and windows open and close with ease.

- **A multiple bit screwdriver.** This type of screwdriver has different types of bits that screw on and off, which makes it convenient for do-it-yourself projects. However, as with the hammer, if you decide that you may be doing a lot of construction projects yourself, you may want to consider investing in an actual screwdriver set for longevity and more precision.

- **An adjustable crescent wrench.** Buy both a smaller and larger one. Certain projects will call for each.

- **A cordless drill.** A cordless drill packs power and saves a lot of time, frustration, and muscle. It also does double duty as both a drill and a screwdriver. You will find yourself reaching for this tool frequently, so invest in a quality one. It is also a good idea to invest in a basic set of drill bits and driver heads as well.

- **A few extension cords and at least one surge protector.** Most power tools come with either four or six-foot cords, which can prove to be a bit frustrating when you are working in a twenty-foot room with one outlet on the other side of the room from where you need it to be. An extension cord is an easy way to remedy this problem and save you a lot of frustration. Since the electricity in many older houses can be a bit temperamental if the house has not been rewired or updated in a long time, particularly when it comes to the usage of power tools, a surge protector is also a very inexpensive way to avoid a big headache.

- **A tool belt or apron.** Although these items may seem hardcore, you will get tired lugging tools around and having to continuously stop what you are doing or climbing up and down ladders in order to switch out or retrieve tools. A tool belt or apron allows you to keep everything within reach and switch out with ease.

- **A pair of tile cutters.** Before all is said and done, you will have the art of cutting tile mastered. Although you can rent tile cutters from your local home improvement store as well as a tile shop, purchasing a pair of your own will be well worth it. Since successfully cutting tile is highly dependent upon recognizing a specific feel, having your own set of cutters saves you the headache of having to familiarize with the way a pair of tile cutters handles every time you begin a new tiling job.

- **A tile saw.** Like the tile cutters, this can be rented. However, it is much more convenient to have your own tools when you will be doing frequent tiling jobs on your own.

- **Several large plastic buckets.** These buckets can be used for everything from mixing paint to filling with water for mopping and cleaning to storing tools.

- **A set of pliers.** Pliers can be used to cut wires and thin metal.

- **Eight and sixteen foot ladders.** The eight-foot ladder is ideal for most indoor projects, and the sixteen-foot ladder will serve most outdoor needs. Make sure you invest in sturdy ladders that lock into place.

- **A caulking gun.** Although you can save the hassle of purchasing caulking guns in bulk for large projects, it is always a good idea to have one on hand for smaller projects and repairs.

- **A device for measuring angles.** Although the official tool of the construction world is a speed square, a good old-fashioned protractor from the office supply section of any supermarket works just a well in a pinch.

You will find that as you become more skilled and enjoy doing some projects more than others enjoy, you will begin to amass tools that are more specialized. You will almost certainly purchase an electronic saw at some point. Some people who are particularly fond of painting will purchase high powered paint machines while others prefer electronic nail guns or carpet cleaners. After doing a few projects, you may find that even though tiling is a perfectly doable task for the average do-it-yourselfer, that you just do not enjoy it and would rather hire a contractor to do tiling jobs in order to free up your time and energy to do other projects. To this degree, the remainder of your toolbox will depend upon your personal likes and dislikes, as well as whatever project you may be doing at the time. However, the above list of items will give you a good base of tools to keep on hand for practical purposes.

Many people who are somewhat adept at do it yourself projects decide to pursue a career in flipping, because they assume their home improvement expertise makes them ideal for buying and renovating properties. However, the actual rehabbing is only part of the real estate process and the construction itself an even smaller part. Although your building and decorating skills may help you, your business will not be successful if you concentrate only on that part and neglect the other tasks that must be done. If you enter the world of buying and selling houses for the sole benefit of being able to renovate houses, because it is something that you like to do and are good at, consider finding a partner to assume the administrative aspects of your business if that is an area in which you are weak or have no interest. This will ensure that your priorities remain balanced and increase your chances of success. Ultimately, this may affect your profit, but the cons balance in guaranteeing your ability to complete the current project and securing future ones.

If you have ever purchased supplies from a home improvement store, then you are also aware that, once the supplies are bought and paid for, there is the issue of transporting them. Obviously, you might be able to put a few cans of paint and other smaller, miscellaneous supplies into the back seat or trunk of a compact car, but lumber, doors, and large boxes that contain fixtures, ceiling fans, or other objects can be somewhat of a problem. Some home improvement stores have a rental truck or trailer available for transporting these materials. If you plan to do a minimum amount of work that would require larger supplies, such as lumber, this may be the most sensible option, because you will only need a vehicle in order to transport your supplies and materials occasionally and for a brief period of time. However, if you will be doing a lot of projects yourself or will be in the habit of furnishing your own supplies or materials, you may want to consider trading in your small, fuel-efficient car for a larger truck or SUV that is capable of hauling larger, heavier items on a regular basis. Although your payments will be higher, they will pay for themselves in the trade off of not having to pay repeatedly to rent a vehicle to transport your home improvement store or gardening center purchases. Additionally, if you should decide to purchase a vehicle for your investment and flipping business, the IRS currently allows tax deductions for automobiles purchased solely for doing business, so it will be possible to recoup some of your additional expenses at the end of the year in the form of a hefty deduction.

CREATING A TIMELINE

Once you assume a property, do not spend a lot of time just sitting on it. Have a plan of entry ready. Once the house is yours, move in, and get going. Aside from a basic timeline, prepare to have a dumpster delivered as soon as the closing is over. You may actually want to arrange for this prior to the closing. Then, clean the house. Literally, go through, clean, and gut it. Get rid of any garbage inside the house, outside the house, around the house, or on the property. If the house has not been occupied in quite a while prior to your taking ownership and the yard and landscaping are particularly overgrown, go ahead, make a few passes over the lawn with a mower, and begin doing some pruning. Clean the outside as well as the inside.

A common mistake of countless rookie flippers is drastically underestimating the amount of time it will take to renovate a piece of property. It is easy to get swept up in the idea of a fast, easy profit. Nevertheless, undervaluing necessary work in one's imagination will not lessen the amount of repair and improvement a project needs in reality. Take the time to design a timeline that is realistic to your budget and the amount of work that must be done. Budgeting too little time is essentially the same as not budgeting at all.

When creating a timeline for your project, budget more time than you think you will need. Finishing a couple of weeks ahead of schedule is usually preferable to finishing a couple of weeks behind. Also, when creating your timeline, be sure to make the appropriate adjustments for DIY and contract projects. A professional painter, for instance, will be able to paint the outside of the average 1,500-2,000 square foot house in 6-8 hours. For the average weekend warrior, though, it will probably take twice that amount of time.

Another thing to consider is the progression of the work. If you will not be occupying the property, then it will be possible to have work simultaneously taking place in all parts of the house, since no one's lifestyle is being disrupted. However, if you will be living on-site while renovations are taking place, this is a bit trickier, and chances are, it is going to take somewhat longer to complete the project because of the logistics. You are more or less going to need to divide the property into quadrants and schedule the work so that it occurs in one (or two if you have a smaller family) quadrant at a time. You will live in the other quadrants, in the meantime, and then shift when the time comes to work in the remaining quadrants. This usually involves not just the mere movement of people, but also the movement of personal items, tools, and supplies, which takes time.

If the kitchen will be renovated in a property in which you will be occupying during renovations, either begin or end with it. Since the kitchen is usually the most essential room in the house, you will need it in working order for the majority of the project. If the kitchen is in good working order when you move in, save it for last. If there are some essential repairs that must completed, begin with those. In general, a rule of thumb that seems to work well is to figure fifteen minutes of labor hours for every square foot of space, assuming that you are renovating from floor to ceiling and that there are no extensive projects, such as redoing plumbing or rewiring electricity, that need to be done. This means that you should expect to spend about fifty hours working on a two hundred square foot kitchen. Keep in mind that not all of this work will be labor intensive or require the work of a professional. This includes small projects such as changing out the hardware on cabinets, cleaning, etc.

You will need to have a serviceable bathroom throughout the duration of a renovation, which can be tricky if there is only one bathroom in the house, and it needs repairs. If you plan to add a bathroom to the property, budget the time to do that first. Then, you will be able to use the new one while the old one is being renovated. If the existing bathroom will remain the sole one in the house, chances are that there is not going to be any way around your being forced to either check into a hotel or stay with a friend or family member for a couple of days. Of course, if the bathroom is more or less in useable condition and you have not budgeted any major projects for it, then this will be somewhat of a non-issue for your timeline.

When you create a timeline for a house that you will be occupying during construction and divide it into quadrants, be sure that the quadrants are large enough to provide appropriate living space for your family. Two people can feasibly live within the confines of two rooms for a couple of weeks, for instance, but a family of five cannot. The stress of being forced to live in cramped conditions for an extended length of time combined with the tension of living in a construction site that is constantly being invaded by strangers and workers can become too much for many families, especially those with younger children or teenagers. Therefore, it is important to give your family enough space to be able to separate, if not spread out, and a place where everyone can blow off steam.

Another important aspect of your timeline, if the property is one that you will not be occupying during renovations, is the burden of the additional mortgage. How long can you realistically afford to pay two mortgages before you find yourself in financial trouble? If it is imperative for you to have the project completed and finished before the first mortgage payment is due, then you are going to be working under a considerably more restrictive timeline than someone who can afford to make a mortgage payment or two before the budget starts to get tight. However, it is important to consider the amount of time you will need to complete your projects. Is it realistic to expect that everything can be completed before the first payment is due? If not, then you should start reorganizing your finances now and make the appropriate adjustment to your timeline. It is better to plan enough time and expect to make the first payment, than to proceed and hope for the best only for your goals not to be realized. You will find yourself dealing with a lot less stress, too.

When creating your timeline, be sure to verify with your contractors that they can complete the work within the dates that you have specified. Many contractors will give you a quote with a time frame, only to pick up additional work between the time you first discussed a project with them and the time your work begins. When you talk to them, be sure you specify any restrictions, such as noise ordinances there may be in your area that may affect their ability to work. The only way for them to give you a fair assessment of the time it will take them to complete a project is for them to know what obstacles may prevent them from delivering. If you do not give them this information and they are unable to complete their work within your timeline because of it, it is your fault not theirs, because you are the project manager. You are responsible for making sure all parties involved have all pertinent information.

When budgeting time for your DIY projects, be sure to allow a margin for error. Even the most seasoned do-it-yourself experts make mistakes. It is completely natural and expected. Since you are not a professional who does this type of work every day, you will be susceptible to the occasional inaccurate measurements, misjudgments, and all-out bad decisions. Using caution and moving at a slightly slower pace will help ensure that these types of errors are minimal in their impact to both your timeline and budget. However, part of successful flipping is realizing that these types of incidents can and do happen and being prepared for them when they do.

While you must consider that every day you hold the property is detracting from your budget, shoddy work and shady contractors can cost you more in the end. Take the time to interview contractors about their experience. Check their references, and get commitments from them in writing. Establish a contractor-specific timeline in your contract for each and every project that you will be hiring out. Not only will this help you stay on track with your budget, but it will also help you coordinate the renovation.

Sample Timeline for a Project
(Assuming a mix of DIY and Contractor work)

	DAY 1	DAY 2	DAY 3	DAY 4	DAY 5	DAY 6
WEEK 1	Appt with kitchen designer to determine new kitchen design and order cabinets.	Disconnect old appliances and place in dumpster; remove old counter tops and vanity; remove ceiling fans and old light fixtures.	Remove old crown and base molding and carpet; make appointment for electrician to repair all electrical problems and plumber to check bathroom plumbing.	Patch walls, remove outlet covers, and prime over red walls in dining room; make appointment for landscape; edge windows with painters' tape; wash down all other walls and allow to dry.	Take down old kitchen cabinets; remove old bathroom vanity; clean tile grout in bathroom.	Visit tile and flooring store to choose new tile for front entryway and hardwood for living room.

	DAY 1	DAY 2	DAY 3	DAY 4	DAY 5	DAY 6
WEEK 2	Make final decision about paint color. Meet with electrician at 1 p.m.	Apply first coat of paint to walls.	Sand woodwork; apply second coat of paint to walls.	Visit store to purchase new appliances.	Stain woodwork; scrub bathtub and tiles; dig out grout that could not be cleaned and regrout.	Initial consultation with landscaper in the a.m.; pick up new shower in the afternoon.
WEEK 3	Siding contractor set to arrive in a.m.	Install new tub and shower in a.m.; Tour garden center with landscaper in the afternoon to choose stones for flower beds and walkways.	Pick up new tile and flooring; begin laying flooring in living and dining rooms.	Continue laying flooring in bedrooms; landscaper arrives to begin digging up old yard and laying sod.	Begin re-installing crown molding and trim; install new light fixtures; visit home improve-ment store to purchase new hardware for bathroom and kitchen cabinets.	Kitchen cabinets to be delivered by noon; plumber coming to hook up toilet in master bath and readjust pipes under kitchen sink; new kitchen countertop arrives.
WEEK 4	Kitchen cabinets arrive in a.m.; paint bathroom.	Landscaper planting flower beds; contractor installing new kitchen cabinets and countertop.	Lay kitchen floor and begin tiling front entry way; new appliances being delivered in p.m.	Grout front entry; install new appliances; begin cleaning and packing away tools.	Hang new house numbers; install new kitchen and bathroom hardware; landscaper installing new walkways.	Clean all floors and wipe down all new cabinets and counter-tops; clean windows and mirrors.

Always remember that a timeline is a live document. Chances are, you will need to make some adjustments and that most projects almost never go exactly as they are initially laid out on paper. The idea is that you have a well thoughtout plan of execution and that you have considered each action that must be completed before beginning the next. Notice, too, that the above sample is based only on a six-day week. If you happen to purchase property in an area that does not at least restrict construction to specific hours each day, thereby limiting the amount of work you can complete on a daily basis, you will find that you will still need at least one day out of each week to rest and recoup from the events of the week. You will also find that many contractors will charge a premium to work on weekends, and many will not work on Sundays at all. Of course, large projects will call for bigger and more detailed timelines, but the principle is still the same.

TAKING OWNERSHIP OF A PROPERTY THAT IS CURRENTLY OCCUPIED

At some point in your career, you may take ownership of a property that is currently occupied. In every state, existing tenants have legal rights, unless you have assumed a property in which the tenant is the previous owner on whom the lending institution foreclosed. In that situation, the occupants are merely squatting. It is important that you understand the rights of existing tenants prior to serving them notice of your intent for the property. If possible, only evict if you have to. If you can, work around existing occupants until their current lease expires. It is usually in the best interest of everyone involved. In many cases, if you have taken ownership of a building that is already a multiple unit building, such as an apartment building, you will have to give the existing occupants the first option to buy. If you cannot work around the existing tenants of a property that you intend to renovate, it is ethical to give them adequate time to relocate. Remember that even though you are now the rightful owner of the property, that property was and is still someone's home.

You may find that, in many cases, most, if not all, of the existing tenants have already begun searching for new homes, because they have been well aware of the developments concerning the ownership of the property as relayed to them either by the previous owner or by their own observation. In those cases, it is very likely that you will not face much opposition to your intentions with the building. Those tenants who have remained have done so with knowledge of the possibility that they may be asked to move and merely made the decision to wait it out on the off chance that the new owner would permit them to stay.

If you do plan to renovate the existing units and sell them, go ahead and give the existing tenants the first option to purchase, whether it is legally required of you or not. This will make them feel as though they are still being valued and give the opportunity for those who ultimately wish to remain in the building the opportunity to do so. Advise them that they may need to relocate for a period of time while you renovate their unit, or if you will be refurbishing the building in segments, you may consider negotiating with them to relocate temporarily to another unit within the building while you work on theirs. Either way, the rate and order that existing tenants vacate a multiple unit building may have an effect on your project timeline, so be sure to keep this in mind when you are planning.

If you must evict, there is a legal process in virtually every geographic region. Most often, you must first give the tenants notice that you wish for them to leave and allow them a specified amount of time to vacate voluntarily. If they refuse, then you can begin the legal process, which usually involves a court appearance during which the tenants are given a window of either thirty or sixty days to vacate before a judge will order the police to come escort them out. Eviction is usually a drawn out and expensive process, so only resort to it when you have exhausted all other forms of recourse.

Another issue you may encounter is assuming a property in which the previous owners have vacated due to foreclosure or eviction but for whatever reason, typically expenses, left behind much of their furniture or belongings. Normally, unless there was some sort of clause in your purchase agreement that stated otherwise, whenever you purchase a home, everything in it becomes yours. This includes any belongings of any previous owners or tenants who may have met with financial trouble that forced them to leave most of their possessions behind, because they simply did not have the money to rent a truck to haul them away by their move out or eviction deadline. Sometimes, you will be approached by these former tenants or owners with a request to obtain their possessions. Although whatever is in the house now legally belongs to you, morally and ethically, it is usually a good idea to give the former occupants the opportunity to remove whatever they wish prior to disposing of the remnants yourself. Again, it must be emphasized that when a situation like this occurs, chances are that the previous owners or tenants have already experienced some level of misfortune that have stripped them of some amount of dignity and left them in an unfortunate situation. A bit of empathy from the new owner will at least ease their anxiety and lessen the pain of the trauma. You do not have to be an all-out philanthropist, but a bit of empathy can be invaluable.

REHABBING FOR THE BUYER MARKET

The essential thing to remember about flipping houses is that you are improving the home to suit potential buyers, not yourself. You may prefer top of the line stainless steel appliances in the kitchen, for instance, but buyers looking for homes in the area in which your property is located may not be willing to pay the added expense for a house with stainless steel appliances. When renovating a home in a neighborhood about which you are largely unfamiliar, look for other houses for sale in the area that are retail quality and attend their open houses. Get a good sense of what amenities houses in the area have. Then, target those same features in your renovation. It is also important to keep things neutral. From floors to wall color, using extreme anything, while it may appeal to some, will significantly narrow your pool of potential buyers.

A big factor in successful renovations is your comprehension of how improvements translate to the homebuyer. Understanding where to spend your money and why is essential. Improvements seldom translate dollar for dollar. In other words, purchasing top of the line appliances for the kitchen may not automatically maximize your potential profit base. If comparable properties in the area have nice, but not top of the line appliances, prospective buyers may not necessarily be able to justify spending the additional cash to purchase your home simply because they can have appliances that they may not value all that highly to begin with.

Understand the market in your chosen area of focus. Tour other open houses to get an idea of the quality of typical homes that go on the market in the area. Of course, as previously discussed, simply investing more money into a property also does not necessarily mean that buyers will be willing to meet your final asking price if it is too far over the standard range for the area.

In today's real estate market, studies have shown that the most important features that most buyers look for in a house are kitchens, master baths, and closet space. Therefore, it makes sense to focus a large portion of your renovation budget on these three areas. Even if you must skimp elsewhere, allocate about 60 percent of your budget to the kitchen and bath areas, because these are the areas in which your potential buyers will be looking at closely.

Your interior improvements should conform to commonly accepted standards of the day. However, it is not usually a good idea to attempt to overdo what can typically be expected within the neighborhood. Doing so will not guarantee you a return on your investment, which may mean that you will be spending money that could be better allocated elsewhere.

For the interior of the house, hardwood floors, stainless steel appliances, and closet organizing systems are the hot choices of the moment in virtually every neighborhood. Hardwood floors often give the interior of a home uniformity and the illusion of a clean, well flowing space. Stainless steel appliances appear top of the line, even if they are not necessarily deluxe models. Closet organizing systems can make small closets appear much larger by maximizing the amount of useable storage space.

Stick to more neutral colors for paint and tiling. Although you may like bright green walls, many buyers may not, and remember that you are not renovating for yourself. You are making improvements to maximize your profit.

Ensure that the improvements you make are keeping with the style of the house. French country can seem somewhat off in a decidedly Spanish style home. Not only is keeping the renovation close to the original style of a home more aesthetically pleasing, it is often easier on the budget. You can usually save money by working to capitalize on the natural feel of a house.

Curb appeal is another important factor. If the house is ugly on the outside, buyers are not going to be very open to the inside. If your property needs external attention, do not overlook it. Sometimes a house needs only a fresh coat of paint or even new landscaping to improve its curb appeal. Other times, more extreme improvements, such as new siding, are needed. Although residing a house is costly, it can also be worth it. This is the type of issue that should be evaluated when you decide whether a piece of property is a good investment or not. Once you have made the decision to buy, do not go back on your decision in an effort to save a little bit of cash. In the end, it will only end up costing you.

Evaluate the current landscaping layout of the house. Is there overgrowth or a tree that has outgrown the space available for it in the yard? Although large trees can sometimes only seem like pesky obstacles that hide natural light, they can actually cause extreme structural damage if the roots grow large enough to cause cracks in the foundation. Sometimes, in addition to improving a home's curb appeal, you can actually contribute to its stability by removing large trees that have grown too close to the house.

Avoid loud, bold colors on the exterior of your house. Research has shown that buyers actually respond best to yellow and neutral-colored homes. If you insist upon using fire engine red or electric blue, use it sparingly. Painting the front door is a great way to add a splash of color that does not leave an impression that is too aggressive to most buyers.

Conform to the demographics of the neighborhood. Painting all of the walls white and installing light colored carpet that will easily reflect dirt and stains is probably not a good idea in a family-oriented neighborhood in which most of your potential buyers will probably have small children. People shopping for homes in this type of area are going to be looking for a color scheme that will camouflage stains and dirt and flooring that will stand up to plenty of wear and tear. In short, they will be looking for a family-friendly home. If buyers expect to find family-friendly homes in a family-friendly neighborhood, you should renovate a property to standards that fit into those guidelines, or it may even be detrimental to your ability to sell the property and ultimately affect your profits. You may find that you are forced to lower the asking price in order to attract buyers, because prospective purchasers may not be willing to pay full price for a home in which they are going to have to repaint the walls and lay new flooring, if they even have the time or the desire to do any work at all.

If you are renovating a multiple unit property, be sure to keep some sense of uniformity within the units. Although prospective condo buyers will want some distinctive differences between their unit and the others in the building, they will equally be repulsed by a property in which the units are so drastically different as to appear poorly planned and haphazard. Consider any outdated aspect of the condominiums that should probably be updated. Since many condominiums do not have high resale values, it is important, if you can, to add some sort of perks to the units when you renovate to attract buyers who may not otherwise be interested in purchasing a condo.

10

FROM INVESTMENT TO FLIP—THE ART OF SHOWING AND SELLING

Now you have finished your improvements, and you are ready to sell the house. This is the big moment you have been waiting for, because, after all, you have not completed the flip until the property sells. Selling a house is a multi-step process. There are several factors to consider, some of which you should give at least some consideration in the early stages of your timeline and planning process. Should you hire an agent to sell the home for you, or will you act as your own agent? Acting as your own agent will save you the commission you will have to pay to an agent, but a professional may be able to use his or her expertise to sell your property more quickly, which, in the long run, may actually save you money. To whom do you market the property? Is your finished product better suited for those retail buyers in search of that great family home, or does it still possess some potential that could be tapped into by a fellow investor? Part of selling quickly is successfully tapping into the right market for the property. Understanding who may best benefit from purchasing the house and why is essential to the time equals money principle. The following is a series of decisions that must be made before you should expect to begin receiving offers from potential buyers who are eager to own your house.

AGENT VERSUS PRIVATE SELLING

A lot of would-be flippers become a bit money hungry at this stage and attempt to act as their own agent in an effort to avoid spending some of their profit on the commission of a professional. This can be both costly and unwise. Real estate agents are trained to market houses. They know how to present them in a manner that showcases their maximum appeal to potential buyers. An agent is also often a member of a large network of buyers and sellers and will, therefore, have more outreach capabilities than you will. If the property you are attempting to sell happens to be in an area that is in such high demand that houses generally sell themselves on reputation of the neighborhood alone, then it may be okay to act as your own agent, as long as you have done your homework on real estate law.

When determining whether to utilize the services of an agent to sell a property, it is also important to consider the amount of time and effort that may become involved in selling a house. Although every investor dreams of receiving a pile of offers during an open house, sometimes the reality is that selling a piece of property at the price you want to sell at can take weeks or even months. During this period, you will be solely responsible for marketing the home and highlighting it in a positive light to potential buyers if you choose to act as your own agent. This time will be taking you away from pursuing your next flip. Although a career in real estate calls for a person of many talents, it does not require someone of all talents. In fact, probably the most important skill of any good entrepreneur is recognizing when you have exceeded your area of expertise and crossed the boundary into another profession at which you are not skilled enough to perform adequately the necessary duties without the expertise of a trained professional. Seeking the assistance of a professional agent in selling your property is neither compromising yourself as a real estate investor nor compromising your profits. It is maximizing them through the utilization of the skills of a professional when and where needed.

If you decide to seek the services of an agent, be sure both you and the agent are clear about the terms of the agreement. You will be asked to sign a formal contract, which specifies the amount of time the realtor will be representing you in an effort to sell the property. You should read your agent's contract very carefully before signing to ensure that it also includes the agent's commission, the price of the home, those appliances that will and will not be included with the house, your responsibilities, the agent's responsibilities, an explanation of the presentation of offers, length of notice for showing the property, and an explanation of how earnest money will be relayed to you.

Remember that once you hire an agent to sell your home, that task becomes his job, which means he is going to have to have access to your home, perhaps on a regular basis. This means that your agent will need a key to your property and, as outlined in the terms of your agreement, may provide you with a sometimes very short notice that he will be bringing prospective buyers to show the home. In many agreements, the notice given to show the home is mere hours. If you will not be living in the property you are attempting to sell, you will not find this to be a huge inconvenience. In fact, you will have little involvement other than doing some basic polishing such as sweeping and dusting every week in order to keep the house from looking as though it has been sitting abandoned for an unspecified length of time. However, if you occupy the property, you will need to make a concentrated effort to keep the house presentable virtually around the clock and should be prepared to vacate for a brief amount of time on short notice.

If you should choose to act as your own agent, there are several essential tasks that you should be prepared to perform.

- Arrange for advertisement of the property in local newspapers and periodicals. This often involves several phone calls and faxes. Many publications will also ask that you create your own classified ad for the property. This must be done in a style that is catchy and sells while still providing interested parties with essential information such as the number of bedrooms and bathrooms.

- Respond to all inquiries regarding your property in a timely manner. Failing to efficiently return phone calls or respond to messages sends a signal that you are not a motivated seller, and that may scare off some of your best potential leads.

- Set up appointments and show the property. This may also include hosting additional open houses. You will be responsible for creating and distributing fact sheets about the property.

- You will need to negotiate offers with potential buyers and ensure all paperwork is accurately completed, signed, and returned to the appropriate parties.

Essentially, you should be prepared to add the title of full-time real estate professional to your repertoire until the house is sold. Since each day the house goes unsold is chipping away at your profit, the more motivated you are to sell the house, the better chance you will have of achieving your desired profit when acting as your own agent.

Unfortunately, this also means that if one of the reasons for pursuing a career in real estate was to have more free time, you will temporarily be juggling two professions instead of one. This will also mean sacrifices to your personal life and family. Although acting as your own agent may save you some money, once you think matters through, you may decide that the freedom to pursue your career of choice as a real estate investor is more than worth the additional expenses of having a real estate professional sell your property for you.

SHOULD I MARKET TO INVESTORS OR RETAIL BUYERS?

When you acquire a new property as an investor, you are faced with two decisions when deciding who your target customer will be. Either you can market to other investors, or you can market to retail buyers. Marketing to other investors is somewhat trickier than marketing to retail buyers, because other investors will only be interested in your property if there is enough room for them to earn a profit from its resale. If you can earn a profit from putting just enough work into a house to improve its value enough to earn a profit from the resale, yet still leave room for other investors to gain from further improvements, then you may wish to pursue a career in this field. Although this is flipping, in a sense, this method is also known to many as fluffing. Essentially, you have done just enough to a house to make it appealing to someone else. If you have, however, spent the last month or month and a half and a significant amount of money bringing a home up to retail standards, then you will want to target retail buyers. Your approach, naturally, is going to be different with each type of buyer.

Investors tend to have a no-frills approach. They are only interested in the bottom line or potential bottom line. Therefore, marketing to them will mostly involve showcasing the potential pot of gold that can be derived from the improvement of the property. Even though it sounds somewhat backwards in a sense, you should point out what is wrong with the house and how improving it will increase its retail value. In this situation, it is wise to do your homework before attempting to sell to another investor. Chances are, he has done his. If possible, get appraisal values on other homes in the area that have had similar work done. For example, if a house down the street with a deck added onto the back recently sold, but the property you have does not have a deck, find out what value the deck had, if any, in the sale of the other house. Assuming it did add value, be prepared to share that with any potential investors to whom you market the house.

Retail buyers, however, are not going to be too interested in how the house can be improved. Instead, they are going to be looking for ways in which a house fits their needs. If they do not need a deck, it is not going to be immediately important to them that the house does not have a deck or that adding one could improve the value of the house. They may become interested in those details at a future point, but you are attempting to sell your house now. So, familiarize yourself with the desires of retail buyers in your area, and highlight those aspects of the house that they find appealing.

The amount of work you have put into a house is going to be your primary determinant of your marketing approach. Obviously, if you spend several weeks and thousands of dollars improving a home to move-in condition, there is probably going to be little, if any, more profit for a fellow investor to usurp from assuming the property for the purpose of immediately reselling. However, there is a subgroup of investors in the world of real estate who primarily seek out long-term investment properties. It is to this crowd that your newly refurbished property may appeal, particularly if it is located in an area that is on the brink of renaissance. Investors earn their livings from being able to somewhat discern outcomes based on the current information available, and a careful and observant one might envision themselves attaching an even more attractive price tag to your property five or ten years down the road. Marketing to this type of investor does have its merits.

Primarily, working deals with long-term investors sets up the win-win situation for which everyone in real estate should be theoretically striving. You are able flip the house in a short amount of time for a considerable profit, and the investor to whom you sell is able to assume a property for which he or she may one day reap a pretty penny without the expense, stress, and woes of a large-scale construction project. Other investors are also less likely to negotiate or bid sentimentally. Your property is an investment to them. For them, deciding whether or not to purchase is a matter of determining potential risk versus profit margin, whereas the decisions of many retail buyers may very well come down to how well they can envision little Suzy living in the upstairs nursery or little Johnny playing baseball in the backyard. This means that if you can back up your claim that the property you are sitting on is a real gem of a find with numbers and statistics, the response you receive from other potential investors may be more favorable than what you may get from retail buyers. Sharing that you initially purchased the property for $65,000, put another $30,000 worth of work into it, and are now asking them to pay $150,000 for your $95,000 investment six weeks later, is probably not the best strategy to use with most retail buyers. However, it might be good information to share if you are attempting to market the home to other investors, because they are going to be interested in your numbers, particularly when it comes time for them to calculate some numbers of their own.

There are, of course, drawbacks to marketing to other investors as well. Since you are an investor and sought out the property yourself, you know that real estate is a shrewd business. Everyone wants to get something out of the deal and investors, above all, need to feel that their money is well vested in its current project. Not only do they need to feel that they are walking away from the negotiation with something, they also need to feel that they still have room to build upon their current situation in order to earn even more. What this essentially translates to in situational matters is that you are probably not going to be able to convince an investor to pay as much for your property as you would a retail buyer, simply because a fellow investor knows your game. Likewise, if you plan to market to fellow investors, you should be prepared to provide vital information pertaining to the lot and structure of the house. A fellow investor is going to be a lot more concerned with the basic bones of your property and whether or not they will contribute to its longevity and adaptability and a lot less caught up in the paint color of the living room and kitchen. Another investor knows that paint color can be changed quickly and inexpensively, but structural adjustments cannot.

A fellow investor, too, is probably going to be more critical of the work you have done to a piece of property than the average retail buyer is. Investors will notice immediately if you have attempted to cut corners in places where you probably should not have and will likely make note of it for negotiation purposes. Therefore, it is a good idea to give some amount of consideration to whether or not you intend to market to investors or retail buyers when you first determine your budget and what work to do. Although you may be able to get away with a few shortcuts with the retail buying market, saving a few dollars in the short term will probably cost you thousands in the long run, if you plan to market to fellow investors. The one exception to this rule of thumb is those investors who intend to purchase the property for the purpose of using it as a rental property. Most landlords are not concerned with or even desirous of top quality appliances and craftsmanship in a house or building they intend to use as a rental property, because they will already be budgeting for wear and tear replacement every few years. Under those circumstances, high-end products are actually detrimental to the deal, because they are more expensive to replace.

STAGING OPEN HOUSES

It sounds odd, but seeing a house is sometimes not enough to convince potential buyers to purchase it. House hunters are looking for a home and a place where they feel comfortable. However, some individuals are better visionaries than others, which means sometimes you will need to provide some source of encouragement to get their creative juices flowing. The best way to do this in an open house is to present your house as a home. Make it feel as cozy and as lived in as possible. If possible, stage the home with furniture. Bake cookies so that the when guests walk in, they will be stimulated by their sense of smell as well as sight.

It is important to be personable during your open house. You want potential buyers to feel at ease while touring the house and comfortable enough to ask questions. Be prepared to answer questions, as well. Have your paperwork organized and easily accessible. Try organizing files on the countertop in the kitchen that are labeled appropriately, so that any answers you do not know off the top of your head can be easily accessed. These types of details, although they are not directly related to your work on the house, demonstrate to potential buyers that you take your business very seriously and will build confidence that you have put the same attentiveness into the work on the house.

Hold your open house on a weekend, if possible, and advertise in more than one local newspaper. If possible, hold your event on a Sunday. Most realtors hold open houses on Sunday afternoons, which means that you will stand a very good chance of pulling potential buyers in who may not have seen your advertisement in addition to those who did. Although it usually costs more to advertise in the Sunday newspaper, it will typically pay off to do so, since most home shoppers regularly determine which open houses they will visit by perusing the Sunday classifieds.

Make sure your ad is clearly marked as an open house. Additionally, you should include pertinent information, such as the number of bedrooms and bathrooms. You may want to include other details that may draw buyers in. For instance, if you went all out renovating the kitchen, you may want to mention that the kitchen is completely new. However, it is not necessary to describe the house in detail. Leave most of the description to the imagination. This will draw curious buyers in as well as keep you from making another classic selling mistake of setting up shoppers for disappointment by over embellishing your home in advertisements. You will also want to include the address, along with brief and clear directions, in your description of the property.

On the day of your open house, make sure there is clear signage pointing the way to the property. If the home is tucked away in a development, include several signs from the main road to the house. Tie balloons to the mailbox, and place a sign clearly in the yard.

Make sure the house is welcoming. Ensure that the house numbers are bold and clearly visible without being overpowering. Place a welcome mat on the front stoop, and ensure that the entry way is well lit. Whenever possible, hold your open house in the mid-afternoon in order to allow as much natural light as possible to flow into the house. Ensure that the house looks homey but not cluttered. If it is cold outside, offer a place for guests to hang their coats. The idea is to provide potential buyers with an environment in which they feel comfortable and can envision themselves at home.

Chances are, most potential buyers who come through your house will be attending more than one open house that day. As anyone who has even been house hunting can attest, it becomes very difficult to distinguish many houses from others. The trick to a quick sale is to make your property the one that stands out.

Be sure to print up plenty of fact sheets, and make sure they are visible and easily accessible to everyone who tours the house. Have your records ready to aid you in answering other inquiries regarding the property that may not be available on the fact sheets. If you are acting as your own agent, be sure to have business cards to pass out to interested parties.

If the weather is rainy on the day of your open house, have a place near the front entry where visitors can store their umbrellas. If the weather is chillier and the house has a useable fireplace, have a fire going. Lay down clear plastic pathways across carpets or floors if you prefer to minimize the impact of heavy traffic flow to new and clean carpet or flooring. Most people will naturally pick up on the hint and stay on the plastic. However, be careful not to make those touring the house feel as if they are too restricted from examining the property thoroughly enough to make a fair determination about it. This will only make them leave in a state of frustration.

Be personable, and appear clean and well put together. Although it may seem that this is understood, clothing and appearance can seem like the least of your worries when you are literally racing against the clock to put finishing paint touches on walls and installing light fixtures mere hours before your open house begins. However, even if you do find your work winding down with the clock, be sure to allow yourself adequate time to bathe and dress appropriately. Having a clean and put together appearance gives you a more professional appearance and lends to your credibility as both a businessperson and a homeowner.

Put away all tools, buckets, and other evidence of recent construction. Most potential buyers prefer to feel as though they are touring a home, not a construction site. Tools and lumbers scraps lying around will give the home an unfinished appearance. If the home has a garage or an attic, neatly store what remaining construction tools or items you have in one of them. They will not affect the opinions of potential buyers when stored in these locations, as most prospective buyers would expect to find those types of items in either of those two places.

Finally, be calm, composed, and friendly throughout the open house. Appearing as though you are under a great amount of stress, are tired, or seem desperate to sell your house could make potential buyers suspicious. It can also affect your negotiation advantage. Remember in earlier chapters, we discussed how to determine when someone is a motivated seller in order to work the best deal. People will not offer you the top dollar that you are expecting if they do not feel they have to. Leaving them with the impression that they can secure the property for a lot less can put an end to your plans for a hefty profit.

ONCE YOU BEGIN RECEIVING OFFERS...

You can be confident that your marketing plan and open houses have been successful once you begin receiving offers.

If all goes well, you will choose from multiple offers. This can sometimes be a bit tricky, because in a world where business is motivated by potential profits, it is easy to follow the impulse to jump on the highest bid. However, this is not always the wisest decision. Consider the terms of each offer, as well. Are any of the prospective buyers asking you to adjust your original terms? If so, how will those ultimately affect your bottom line? Are there any contingencies included in the contract, such as condition of sale of another property or pending lender approval? These are other flags that may shift what may initially seem like the ideal offer to lower in rank. When are the requested closing dates on the offers presented? Remember, your goal as an investor is typically to hold the property for as brief amount of time as possible, because for each month you hold the property, you pay mortgage and maintenance expenses, which ultimately cut into your bottom line.

While evaluating your offers, determine if there is anything that can give one an edge over the others or make it particularly more appealing than any of the choices immediately before you. Then, discuss it with your agent. Tell him or her what terms or stipulations you would like to include as a counteroffer and why. Consider counteroffers carefully before making them, though. Most offers stipulate a deadline for acceptance. If you submit a counteroffer and the deadline for the original offer expires, the buyer then has the option to say no to both the terms of their original offer and your counteroffer. This means that you may be right back to where you started or will be forced to accept a lesser offer. Sometimes the gamble is worth it, but part of the art of selling is to read between the lines of the offers you receive in order to determine how eager potential buyers are to own your property.

Once you determine that you would like to accept a particular offer, be sure to read the fine print before signing. Many shrewd and sly business people will cleverly slip clauses or contingencies into offers in sections in which they know most people only glance over. Check for any conflicting or unrealistic information in the offer. Make sure that the lender-approved terms of the mortgage loan agree with those outlined in the offer. Be sure that you understand any contingency clauses the buyer has placed into the contract, and review them carefully. Consider the impact they could potentially have on you if the buyer exercises them. Most importantly, if you find anything within the terms with which you are uncomfortable, call it forward, and ask for clarification or explanation. As discussed in an earlier chapter, if both parties cannot walk away from the bargaining table feeling as though it is a win-win situation, then it probably is not.

However, it is also equally important to understand that contingencies are seldom placed into an offer to take advantage of the seller. They are more or less a way to protect the buyer from getting lost in a bad investment. When evaluating contingencies, put yourself on both sides of the table. Although it may not exactly be your ideal situation, that does not mean it is not reasonable. If the offer makes sense once you review it from the buyer's perspective, then you should probably give it fair consideration as a good businessperson.

If you can, close quickly once you accept an offer. Remember, the longer you hold the property, the more expenses you incur in association with it. Also, begin thinking of your next flip, if you have not already. As you will recall from the section regarding taxes, you have a brief holding period for designating properties of interest during which your profits from the current flip are free and clear of taxes. Nevertheless, if you sit too long, then the profits become regular income and are subject to normal income tax laws. During the waiting period between the acceptance of the offer and the closing, begin touring potential properties and constructing a short list. If you happen to fall into a great opportunity, you may even begin the purchasing process again, as long as you are careful in your planning and calculations. Be sure that you include a contingency clause in your offer that addresses your own timeline, such as making your offer conditional on the completion of your own closing.

S

SUMMARY OF THE PROGRESSION OF A PROPERTY FLIP

- With a careful balance of research, patience, and strategy, real estate can be a fast-paced career of quick profits. However, achieving your goals requires discipline and business savvy. Learning how to balance your creative visions with a good business sense is essential to achieving success.

- Know what you are getting into and how a career in real estate will affect your life and lifestyle prior to actually purchasing your first property. Have a plan and know in what direction you are headed. Be sure to consider the full consequences of full-time versus part-time ventures. Honestly evaluating your time and what it means to you is a great way to start. Knowing how your new career will affect your family is not only a step in the right direction, but also a good idea for keeping your family intact.

- Being realistic with yourself about how much time and money you can commit to investing is essential, because getting in over your head is one way to put an end to your dreams before you even begin. After you assess your finances, determine what type of investor you will be. Pursuing a career as a dealer will yield you smaller but faster profits with minimal personal involvement. Becoming a retail flipper involves more of your time and money, but it typically results in considerably higher profits.

- Research your target neighborhoods in order to determine the best place for you to begin looking for property in which to invest. Then, spend time and effort getting to know the area. Understand the demographics and know to whom you will be marketing. Determine what homeowners moving into the area expect in a new home. Then, begin to assemble your team and make connections.

- Seek out a lawyer and an accountant with real estate expertise. Begin networking with real estate agents who specialize in the area. Tour open houses to get an idea of the price range as well as what your money will buy in the area. Secure financing and begin searching for your first flip. Once you find it, evaluate the purchase price versus the costs of the renovations you will need to make in order to restore the property to its retail value.

- Once you locate a property you like, negotiate a win-win situation for all, and make an offer. When your offer is accepted, set the closing process in motion. Begin thinking about your project timeline and budget, as well as whether your goal will be to market to retail buyers or other investors. Leave room in your budget for unexpected repairs and expenses. Determine whether you will be doing the improvements yourself or if you will be seeking the assistance of contractors. If you decide to utilize contractors, begin consulting friends, family, and colleagues for references.

- Interview at least three contractors before hiring one. Have your lawyer draw up a contract, ensure all bases are covered, and be sure you have an out in the event that the contractor you hire does not live up to the terms of your contracts. If you will not be living in the property during construction, be sure to visit daily to check the progress of the work. Keep the project on time and within budget as much as possible. Maintain open communication and be sure that you have clearly conveyed your expectations to your contractors and that they are able to interpret them effectively into a finished product.

- As the project nears completion, begin working with your real estate agent to develop a marketing plan, and set dates for an open house. When the day of the open house arrives, be sure the house is staged to appear warm and welcoming. Be sure to post adequate signage so that prospective buyers can locate the house.

- Be warm, friendly, and knowledgeable with prospective buyers. In selling the property, utilize the same negotiation skills you used to purchase it. Be realistic about the high and low price you set in your mind. Once you sell your property, decide in advance on a property or properties you intend to purchase within six weeks, and purchase at least one of them within six months to begin the flipping process again.

CONCLUSION

C

There is no doubt that once you venture into a career in real estate, you will become hooked very quickly. There is a definite adrenaline rush in seeing a piece of property that was in a state of neglect when you assumed it blossom into a showplace. Although it is hard work, the rewards and potential are practically limitless. Many investors will tell you that they actually experience joy in seeing a neglected house brought back to life. For them, each flip is like a work of art, and selling it is like introducing their latest masterpiece to the world. Some even report that they will follow the progress of a particular project after it has been sold. They will maintain relationships with the new owners and visit or drive by on a regular basis to observe new changes or additions.

With each property, you will encounter unique problems that will build on your experience and from which you will walk away with several tricks and tips to add to your repertoire. Many times, you will find yourself outside your comfort zone, and even though it may seem chaotic at first, in time the process will become almost methodical. However, each house is different, and it is amazing to bring out the personality of a piece of property. Do not be discouraged by the little bumps in the road. Few executives can boast that they have never made any mistakes during their career. Learning how to take those bumps and smooth them into success stories is part of the adventure of being an investor.

For many, the most difficult aspect of a career in real estate is overcoming the fear of failure. Even when we have determination, there is always a seed of doubt in the back of even the most confident of minds. Those entrepreneurs who push forward are not able to repress that doubt. They are simply not able to allow it to grow and overcome their dreams. There is some level of risk involved in every venture, and the advice that nearly every successful businessperson will give to the person starting out is to take the risks, sometimes even when others tell you not to.

It is important to maintain your knowledge as you go through your flipping career. The laws regulating real estate are constantly changing and evolving, so it is important to understand that although you will eventually reach a point in which you can operate with confidence, you should never get too comfortable. Inevitably, as soon as you do, a law will change that will have you reevaluating the way in which you conduct business. You can be confident, though, that you will always be challenged and that you will never become bored.

After several years of flipping single-family properties, some investors decide to explore multi-unit ventures. This is a good way to expand your business, but there are some differences between single-family and multi-unit flips. Some investors purchase multi-unit buildings with the actual intention to remodel every unit and then resell them, while others purchase a building with no intention of renovating but simply selling the units off one at a time for a profit. Primarily, if you purchase a building of multiple condominiums and plan to refurbish them, there will be two codes to which you must adhere: the code for the building and the code for individual units. Keep in mind that renovating several condos simultaneously is similar in concept to redoing several single-family properties at the same time. What this means is that while it may be possible to reap a considerably higher profit from the sale of the units of a multi-unit building, it will, in all likelihood, take considerably longer to renovate a building of condominiums.

Many wonder about retirement. In real estate, it is not so much the money aspects that are bothersome, as it is how to find an "out" once you are "in." How do you end your investing career? When you reach that point, chances are that you will have several options. If you are in a corporation, you will need to determine with your partners whether you will retire simultaneously or individually. If you choose to retire in sync, you will be faced with the decision of whether to dissolve the company or sell it. The decision will largely be determined on the state of the corporation at that time and the potential profit you stand to gain from each. If your partners and you determine that you will each retire when each is ready, then it is a good idea to have a plan for how this will be handled. Determine whether the exiting partner will be expected to option his share of the company to the remaining partners or if he may sell it to whom he chooses.

Although it seems almost precarious to be thinking of retirement before one even begins, it is always important to think ahead. Whether it is for breaking into the world of real estate investment, maintaining a successful career in it, or exiting it for a comfortable retirement, have a plan. While it may not be immediately imperative to think of winding down your career, it is still wise to have a plan for how much of your investment profits you will set aside for the future and into what type of account. Will you continuously reinvest, or will you just allow the cash to appreciate in a traditional bank account? Work with your accountant to determine the best plan of action for your future as well as the present.

In every aspect of your life, a little bit of planning and knowledge can take you a long way as a real estate investor. Having vision and being prepared to realize it are the only things you really need to begin in order to move forward. These two qualities can take you virtually as far as you will let them. Be prepared to experience some bumps and bruises along the way, but do not let minor setbacks discourage you. Part of being successful in any venture is adaptability. Remember the qualities that were discussed in the beginning of this book? They are not qualities one merely needs to break into the business, but to remain in it and become successful. They are life qualities.

Once you tap into your potential and establish a rhythm for your business, your possibilities are limitless. Understand that being a good businessperson is a lifestyle as much as a way to conduct transactions. Reward yourself, and avoid investor burnout by taking a breather every now and then. Although flipping houses can become very addicting, do not lose sight of the reasons you decided to go into business for yourself. Perhaps it was to build a respectable retirement or to have more quality time. Give yourself and your family those vacations you have been dreaming about for years. Get away from the world of real estate and try not to imagine how you would renovate your resort if you could. After all, your next flip will be waiting when your vacation ends.

REFERENCE LIST

r

Flipping Properties, Bronchick, William, Dahlstrom, Robert, Dearborn Trade Publishing, 2001.

Financing Secrets of a Millionaire Real Estate Investor, Bronchick, William, Dearborn Trade Publishing, 2003.

Real Estate Flipping Grow Rich Buying and Selling Property, Weiss, Mark B, Adams Media, 2004.

The Complete Guide to Flipping Properties, Berges, Steve, Wiley & Sons Inc, 2004.

Fix It and Flip It, Hamilton, Gene, Hamilton Katie, McGraw Hill Publishing, 2004.

U.S. Census Bureau website
www.census.gov

FHA Website
www.hud.gov

INDEX

A

accountant 43, 44, 45, 84

adjustable mortgages 59, 60

agent 24, 25, 38, 39, 40, 41, 42, 99, 108, 109, 113, 127, 128, 132, 134, 140, 141, 189, 190, 191, 192, 193, 200, 202

amortization 64

attorney 36, 37, 38, 113, 114

auction 108, 112, 130, 131, 132, 133

auction properties 130, 131

B

balloon mortgages 59

bank owned 130

blanket mortgages 60

broker 38, 41, 88

budget 14, 15, 16, 26, 27, 29, 30, 44, 52, 53, 54, 63, 74, 77, 99, 117, 120, 124, 128, 142, 143, 145, 146, 147, 148, 149, 151, 154, 155, 156, 157, 158, 159, 160, 161, 162, 163, 164, 165, 166, 167, 176, 178, 180, 186, 187, 197

business plan 12, 13, 36, 64

GLOSSARY

g

401(k)/403(b) An investment plan sponsored by an employer which enables individuals to set aside pre-tax income for retirement or emergency purposes. 401(k) plans are provided by private corporations. 403(b) plans are provided by non-profit organizations.

401(k)/403(b) loan A type of financing using a loan against the money accumulated in a 401(k)/403(b) plan.

Abatement Sometimes referred to as free rent or early occupancy. A condition that could happen in addition to the primary term of the lease.

Above Building Standard Finishes and specialized designs that have been upgraded in order to accommodate a tenant's requirements.

Absorption Rate The speed and amount of time at which rentable space, in square feet, is filled.

Abstract or Title Search The process of reviewing all transactions that have been recorded publicly in order to determine whether any defects in the title exist which could interfere with a clear property ownership transfer.

Accelerated Cost Recovery System A calculation for taxes to provide more depreciation for the first few years of ownership.

Accelerated Depreciation A method of depreciation where the value of a property depreciates faster in the first few years after purchasing it.

Acceleration Clause A clause in a contract that gives the lender the right to demand immediate payment of the balance of the loan if the borrower defaults on the loan.

Acceptance An approval of a buyer's offer written by the seller.

Ad Valorem A Latin phrase which translates as "according to value." Refers to a tax that is imposed on a property's value which is typically based on the local government's evaluation of the property.

Addendum An addition or update for an existing contract between parties.

Additional Principal Payment Additional money paid to the lender, apart from the scheduled loan payments, to pay more of the principal balance, shortening the length of the loan.

Adjustable Rate Mortgage (ARM) A home loan with an interest rate that is adjusted periodically in order to reflect changes in a specific financial resource.

Adjusted Funds From Operations (AFFO) The rate of REIT performance or ability to pay dividends which is used by many analysts who have concerns about the quality of earnings as measured by Funds From Operations (FFO).

Adjustment Date The date at which the interest rate is adjusted for an Adjustable-Rate Mortgage (ARM).

Adjustment Period The amount of time between adjustments for an interest rate in an ARM.

Administrative Fee A percentage of the value of the assets under management, or a fixed annual dollar amount charged to manage an account.

Advances The payments the servicer makes when the borrower fails to send a payment.

Adviser A broker or investment banker who represents an owner in a transaction and is paid a retainer and/or a performance fee once a financing or sales transaction has closed.

Agency Closing A type of closing in which a lender uses a title company or other firm as an agent to finish a loan.

Agency Disclosure A requirement in most states that agents who act for both buyers or sellers must disclose who they are working for in the transaction.

Aggregation Risk The risk that is associated with warehousing mortgages during the process of pooling them for future security.

Agreement of Sale A legal document the buyer and seller must approve and sign that details the price and terms in the transaction.

Alienation Clause The provision in a loan that requires the borrower to pay the total balance of the loan at once if the property is sold or the ownership transferred.

Alternative Mortgage A home loan that does not match the standard terms of a fixed-rate mortgage.

Alternative or Specialty Investments Types of property that are not considered to be conventional real estate investments, such as self-storage facilities, mobile homes, timber, agriculture, or parking lots.

Amortization The usual process of paying a loan's interest and principal via scheduled monthly payments.

Amortization Schedule A chart or table which shows the percentage of each payment that will be applied toward principal and interest over the life of the mortgage and how the loan balance decreases until it reaches zero.

Amortization Tables The mathematical tables that are used to calculate what a borrower's monthly payment will be.

Amortization Term The number of months it will take to amortize the loan.

Anchor The business or individual who is serving as the primary draw to a commercial property.

Annual Mortgagor Statement A yearly statement to borrowers which details the remaining principal balance and amounts paid throughout the year for taxes and interest.

Annual Percentage Rate (APR) The interest rate that states the actual cost of borrowing money over the course of a year.

Annuity The regular payments of a fixed sum.

Application The form a borrower must complete in order to apply for a mortgage loan, including information

such as income, savings, assets, and debts.

Application Fee A fee some lenders charge that may include charges for items such as property appraisal or a credit report unless those fees are included elsewhere.

Appraisal The estimate of the value of a property on a particular date given by a professional appraiser, usually presented in a written document.

Appraisal Fee The fee charged by a professional appraiser for his estimate of the market value of a property.

Appraisal Report The written report presented by an appraiser regarding the value of a property.

Appraised Value The dollar amount a professional appraiser assigned to the value of a property in his report.

Appraiser A certified individual who is qualified by education, training, and experience to estimate the value of real and personal property.

Appreciation An increase in the home's or property's value.

Appreciation Return The amount gained when the value of the real estate assets increases during the current quarter.

Arbitrage The act of buying securities in one market and selling them immediately in another market in order to profit from the difference in price.

ARM index A number that is publicly published and used as the basis for interest rate adjustments on an ARM.

As-Is Condition A phrase in a purchase or lease contract in which the new tenant accepts the existing condition of the premises as well as any physical defects.

Assessed Value The value placed on a home which is determined by a tax assessor in order to calculate a tax base.

Assessment (1) The approximate value of a property. (2) A fee charged in addition to taxes in order to help pay for items such as water, sewer, street improvements, etc.

Assessor A public officer who estimates the value of a property for the purpose of taxation.

Asset A property or item of value owned by an individual or company.

Asset Management Fee A fee that is charged to investors based on the amount of money they have invested into real estate assets for the particular fund or account.

Asset Management The various tasks and areas around managing real estate assets from the initial investment until the time it is sold.

Asset Turnover The rate of total revenues for the previous 12 months divided by the average total assets.

Assets Under Management The amount of the current market value of real estate assets which a manager is responsible to manage and invest.

Assignee Name The individual

or business to whom the lease, mortgage or other contract has been re-assigned.

Assignment The transfer of rights and responsibilities from one party to another for paying a debt. The original party remains liable for the debt should the second party default.

Assignor The person who transfers the rights and interests of a property to another.

Assumable Mortgage A mortgage that is capable of being transferred to a different borrower.

Assumption The act of assuming the mortgage of the seller.

Assumption Clause A contractual provision that enables the buyer to take responsibility for the mortgage loan from the seller.

Assumption Fee A fee charged to the buyer for processing new records when they are assuming an existing loan.

Attorn To agree to recognize a new owner of a property and to

pay rent to the new landlord.

Average Common Equity The sum of the common equity for the last five quarters divided by five.

Average Downtime The number of months that are expected between a lease's expiration and the beginning of a replacement lease under the current market conditions.

Average Free Rent The number of months the rent abatement concession is expected to be granted to a tenant as part of an incentive to lease under current market conditions

Average Occupancy The average rate of each of the previous 12 months that a property was occupied.

Average Total Assets The sum of the total assets of a company for the previous five quarters divided by five.

Back Title Letter A letter that an attorney receives from a title insurance company before examining the title for insurance purposes.

Back-End Ratio The calculation lenders use to compare a borrower's gross monthly income to their total debt.

Balance Sheet A statement that lists an individual's assets, liabilities and net worth.

Balloon Loan A type of mortgage in which the monthly payments are not large enough to repay the loan by the end of the term, and the final payment is one large payment of the remaining balance.

Balloon Payment The final huge payment due at the end of a balloon mortgage.

Balloon Risk The risk that a borrower may not be able to come up with the funds for the balloon payment at maturity.

Bankrupt The state an individual or business is in if they are unable to repay their debt when it is due.

Bankruptcy A legal proceeding where a debtor can obtain relief from payment of certain obligations through restructuring their finances.

Base Loan Amount The amount which forms the basis for the loan payments.

Base Principal Balance The original loan amount once adjustments for subsequent fundings and principal payments have been made without including accrued interest or other unpaid debts.

Base Rent A certain amount that is used as a minimum rent, providing for rent increases over the term of the lease agreement.

Base Year The sum of actual taxes and operating expenses during a given year, often that in which a lease begins.

Basis Point A term for 1/100 of one percentage point.

Before-Tax Income An individual's income before taxes have been deducted.

Below-Grade Any structure or part of a structure that is below the surface of the ground that surrounds it.

Beneficiary An employee who is covered by the benefit plan his company provides.

Beta The measurement of common stock price volatility for a company in comparison to the market.

Bid The price or range an investor is willing to spend on whole loans or securities.

Bill of Sale A written legal document that transfers the ownership of personal property to another party.

Binder (1) A report describing the conditions of a property's title. (2) An early agreement between seller and buyer.

Biweekly Mortgage A mortgage repayment plan that requires payments every two weeks to help repay the loan over a shorter amount of time.

Blanket Mortgage A rare type of mortgage that covers more than one of the borrower's properties.

Blind Pool A mixed fund that accepts capital from investors without specifying property assets.

Bond Market The daily

buying and selling of thirty-year treasury bonds which also affects fixed rate mortgages.

Book Value The value of a property based on its purchase amount plus upgrades or other additions with depreciation subtracted.

Break-Even Point The point at which a landlord's income from rent matches expenses and debt.

Bridge Loan A short-term loan for individuals or companies that are still seeking more permanent financing.

Broker A person who serves as a go-between for a buyer and seller.

Brokerage The process of bringing two or more parties together in exchange for a fee, commission, or other compensation.

Buildable Acres The portion of land that can be built on after allowances for roads, setbacks, anticipated open spaces, and unsuitable areas have been made.

Building Code The laws set

forth by the local government regarding end use of a given piece of property. These law codes may dictate the design, materials used, and/or types of improvements that will be allowed.

Building Standard Plus Allowance A detailed list provided by the landlord stating the standard building materials and costs necessary to make the premises inhabitable.

Build-Out Improvements to a property's space that have been implemented according to the tenant's specifications.

Build-to-Suit A way of leasing property, usually for commerical purposes, in which the developer or landlord builds to a tenant's specifications.

Buydown A term that usually refers to a fixed-rate mortgage for which additional payments can be applied to the interest rate for a temporary period, lowering payments for a period of one to three years.

Buydown Mortgage A style of home loan in which the lender receives a higher payment in order to convince them to reduce the interest rate during the initial years of the mortgage.

Buyer's Remorse A nervousness first-time homebuyers tend to feel after signing a sales contract or closing the purchase of a house.

Call Date The periodic or continuous right a lender has to call for payment of the total remaining balance prior to the date of maturity.

Call Option A clause in a loan agreement that allows a lender to demand repayment of the entire principal balance at any time.

Cap A limit on how much the monthly payment or interest rate is allowed to increase in an adjustable-rate mortgage.

Capital Appreciation The change in a property's or portfolio's market value after it has been adjusted for capital improvements and partial sales.

Capital Expenditures The purchase of long-term assets,

or the expansion of existing ones which prolongs the life or efficiency of those assets.

Capital Gain The amount of excess when the net proceeds from the sale of an asset are higher than its book value.

Capital Improvements Expenses that prolong the life of a property or add new improvements to it.

Capital Markets Public and private markets where individuals or businesses can raise or borrow capital.

Capitalization The mathematical process that investors use to derive the value of a property using the rate of return on investments.

Capitalization Rate The percentage of return as it is estimated from the net income of a property.

Carryback Financing A type of funding in which a seller agrees to hold back a note for a specified portion of the sales price.

Carrying Charges Costs incurred to the landlord when initially leasing out a property and then during the periods of vacancy.

Cash Flow The amount of income an investor receives on a rental property after operating expenses and loan payments have been deducted.

Cashier's Check A check the bank draws on its own resources instead of a depositor's account.

Cash-on-Cash Yield The percentage of a property's net cash flow and the average amount of invested capital during the specified operating year.

Cash-Out Refinance The act of refinancing a mortgage for an amount that is higher than the original amount for the purpose of using the leftover cash for personal use.

Certificate of Deposit A type of deposit that is held in a bank for a limited time and pays a certain amount of interest to the depositor.

Certificate of Deposit Index (CODI) A rate that is based on interest rates of six-month CDs and is often used to determine interest rates for some ARMs.

Certificate of Eligibility A type of document that the Veterans Administration issues to verify the eligibility of a veteran for a VA loan.

Certificate of Occupancy (CO) A written document issued by a local government or building agency that states that a home or other building is inhabitable after meeting all building codes.

Certificate of Reasonable Value (CRV) An appraisal presented by the Veterans Administration that shows the current market value of a property.

Certificate of Veteran Status A document veterans or reservists receive if they have served 90 days of continuous active duty (including training time).

Chain of Title The official record of all transfers of ownership over the history of a piece of property.

Chapter 11 The part of the federal bankruptcy code that deals with reorganizations of businesses.

Chapter 7 The part of the federal bankruptcy code that deals with liquidations of businesses.

Circulation Factor The interior space that is required for internal office circulation and is not included in the net square footage.

Class A A property rating that is usually assigned to those that will generate the maximum rent per square foot, due to superior quality and/or location.

Class B A good property that most potential tenants would find desirable but lacks certain attributes that would bring in the top dollar.

Class C A building that is physically acceptable but offers few amenities, thereby becoming cost-effective space for tenants who are seeking a particular image.

Clear Title A property title that is free of liens, defects, or other legal encumbrances.

Clear-Span Facility A type of building, usually a warehouse or parking garage, consisting of vertical columns on the outer edges of the structure and clear spaces between the columns.

Closed-End Fund A mixed fund with a planned range of investor capital and a limited life.

Closing The final act of procuring a loan and title in which documents are signed between the buyer and seller and/or their respective representation, and all money, concerned in the contract, changes hands.

Closing Costs The expenses that are related to the sale of real estate including loan, title, and appraisal fees and are beyond the price of the property itself.

Closing Statement See: Settlement Statement.

Cloud on Title Certain conditions uncovered in a title search that present a negative impact to the title for the property.

Commercial Mortgage-Backed Securities (CMBS) A type of securities that is backed by loans on commercial real estate.

Collateralized Mortgage Obligation (CMO) Debt that is fully based on a pool of mortgages.

Co-Borrower Another individual who is jointly responsible for the loan and is on the title to the property.

Cost of Funds Index (COFI) An index used to determine changes in the interest rates for certain ARMs.

Co-Investment Program A separate account for an insurance company or investment partnership in which two or more pension funds may co-invest their capital in an individual property or a portfolio of properties.

Co-Investment The condition that occurs when two or more pension funds or groups of funds are sharing ownership of a real estate investment.

Collateral The property for

which a borrower has obtained a loan, thereby assuming the risk of losing the property if the loan is not repaid according to the terms of the loan agreement.

Collection The effort on the part of a lender, due to a borrower defaulting on a loan, which involves mailing and recording certain documents in the event that the foreclosure procedure must be implemented.

Commercial Mortgage A loan used to purchase a piece of commercial property or building.

Commercial Mortgage Broker A broker specialized in commercial mortgage applications.

Commercial Mortgage Lender A lender specialized in funding commercial mortgage loans.

Commingled Fund A pooled fund that enables qualified employee benefit plans to mix their capital in order to achieve professional management, greater diversification, or investment positions in larger properties.

Commission A compensation to salespeople that is paid out of the total amount of the purchase transaction.

Commitment The agreement of a lender to make a loan with given terms for a specific period.

Commitment Fee The fee a lender charges for the guarantee of specified loan terms, to be honored at some point in the future.

Common Area Assessments Sometimes called Homeowners' Association Fees. Charges paid to the Homeowners' Association by the individual unit owners, in a condominium or Planned Unit Development (PUD), that are usually used to maintain the property and common areas.

Common Area Maintenance The additional charges the tenant must pay in addition to the base rent to pay for the maintenance of common areas.

Common Areas The portions of a building, land, and

amenities, owned or managed by a planned unit development (PUD) or condominium's homeowners' association, that are used by all of the unit owners who share in the common expense of operation and maintenance.

Common Law A set of unofficial laws that were originally based on English customs and used to some extent in several states.

Community Property Property that is acquired by a married couple during the course of their marriage and is considered in many states to be owned jointly, unless certain circumstances are in play.

Comparable Sales Also called Comps or Comparables. The recent selling prices of similar properties in the area that are used to help determine the market value of a property.

Compound Interest The amount of interest paid on the principal balance of a mortgage in addition to accrued interest.

Concessions Cash, or the equivalent, that the landlord pays or allows in the form of rental abatement, additional tenant finish allowance, moving expenses, or other costs expended in order to persuade a tenant to sign a lease.

Condemnation A government agency's act of taking private property, without the owner's consent, for public use through the power of eminent domain.

Conditional Commitment A lender's agreement to make a loan providing the borrower meets certain conditions.

Conditional Sale A contract to sell a property which states that the seller will retain the title until all contractual conditions have been fulfilled.

Condominium A type of ownership in which all of the unit owners own the property, common areas, and buildings jointly, and have sole ownership in the unit to which they hold the title.

Condominium Conversion Changing an existing rental property's ownership to the condominium form of ownership.

Condominium Hotel A condominium project that involves registration desks, short-term occupancy, food and telephone services, and daily cleaning services, and is generally operated as a commercial hotel even though the units are individually owned.

Conduit A strategic alliance between lenders and unaffiliated organizations that acts as a source of funding by regularly purchasing loans, usually with a goal of pooling and securitizing them.

Conforming Loan A type of mortgage that meets the conditions to be purchased by Fannie Mae or Freddie Mac.

Construction Documents The drawings and specifications an architect and/or engineer provides to describe construction requirements for a project.

Construction Loan A short-term loan to finance the cost of construction, usually dispensed in stages throughout the construction project.

Construction Management The process of ensuring that the stages of the construction project are completed in a timely and seamless manner.

Construction-to-Permanent Loan A construction loan that can be converted to a longer-term traditional mortgage after construction is complete.

Consultant Any individual or company that provides the services to institutional investors, such as defining real estate investment policies, making recommendations to advisors or managers, analyzing existing real estate portfolios, monitoring and reporting on portfolio performance, and/or reviewing specified investment opportunities.

Consumer Price Index (CPI) A measurement of inflation, relating to the change in the prices of goods and services that are regularly purchased by a specific population during a certain period of time.

Contiguous Space Refers to several suites or spaces on a floor (or connected floors) in a given building that can be combined and rented to a single tenant.

Contingency A specific condition that must be met before either party in a contract can be legally bound.

Contract An agreement, either verbal or written, to perform or not to perform a certain thing.

Contract documents See: Construction Documents.

Contract Rent Also known as Face Rent. The dollar amount of the rental obligation specified in a lease.

Conventional Loan A long-term loan from a nongovernmental lender that a borrower obtains for the purchase of a home.

Convertible Adjustable-Rate Mortgage A type of mortgage that begins as a traditional ARM but contains a provision to enable the borrower to change to a fixed-rate mortgage during a certain period of time.

Convertible Debt The point in a mortgage at which the lender has the option to convert to a partially or fully owned property within a certain period of time.

Convertible Preferred Stock Preferred stock that can be converted to common stock under certain conditions which have been specified by the issuer.

Conveyance The act of transfering a property title between parties by deed.

Cooperative Also called a Co-op. A type of ownership by multiple residents of a multi-unit housing complex, in which they all own shares in the cooperative corporation that owns the property, thereby having the right to occupy a particular apartment or unit.

Cooperative Mortgage Any loan that is related to a cooperative residential project.

Core Properties The main types of property, specifically office, retail, industrial, and multi-family.

Co-Signer A second individual or party who also signs a promissory note or loan agreement, thereby taking responsibility for the debt in the event that the primary borrower cannot pay.

Cost-Approach Improvement Value The current expenses for constructing a copy or replacement for an existing structure, but subtracting an estimate of the accrued depreciation.

Cost-Approach Land Value The estimated value of the basic interest in the land, as if it were available for development to its highest and best use.

Cost-of-Sale Percentage An estimate of the expenses of selling an investment that represents brokerage commissions, closing costs, fees, and other necessary sales costs.

Coupon The token or expected interest rate the borrower is charged on a promissory note or mortgage.

Courier Fee The fee that is charged at closing for the delivery of documents between all parties concerned in a real estate transaction.

Covenant A written agreement, included in deeds or other legal documents, that defines the requirements for certain acts or use of a property.

Credit An agreement in which a borrower promises to repay the lender at a later date and receives something of value in exchange.

Credit Enhancement The necessary credit support, in addition to mortgage collateral, in order to achieve the desired credit rating on mortgage-backed securities.

Credit History An individual's record which details his current and past financial obligations and performance.

Credit Life Insurance A type of insurance that pays the balance of a mortgage if the borrower dies.

Credit Rating The degree of creditworthiness a person is assigned based on his credit history and current financial status.

Credit Report An individual's record detailing an individual's credit, employment, and residence history used to determine the individual's creditworthiness.

Credit Repository A company that records and updates credit applicants' financial and credit information from various sources.

Credit Score Sometimes called a Credit Risk Score. The number contained in a consumer's credit report that represents a statistical summary of the information.

Creditor A party to whom other parties owe money.

Cross-Collateralization A group of mortgages or properties that jointly secures one debt obligation.

Cross-Defaulting A provision that allows a trustee or lender to require full payment on all loans in a group, if any single loan in the group is in default.

Cumulative Discount Rate A percentage of the current value of base rent with all landlord lease concessions taken into account.

Current Occupancy The current percentage of units in a building or property that is leased.

Current Yield The amount of the coupon divided by the price.

Deal Structure The type of agreement in financing an acquisition. The deal can be unleveraged, leveraged, traditional debt, participating debt, participating/convertible debt, or joint ventures.

Debt Any amount one party owes to another party.

Debt Service Coverage Ratio (DSCR) A property's yearly net operating income divided by the yearly cost of debt service.

Debt Service The amount of money that is necessary to meet all interest and principal payments during a specific period.

Debt-to-Income Ratio The percentage of a borrower's monthly payment on long-term debts divided by his gross monthly income.

Dedicate To change a private property to public ownership for a particular public use.

Deed A legal document that conveys property ownership to the buyer.

Deed in Lieu of Foreclosure A situation in which a deed is given to a lender in order to satisfy a mortgage debt and to avoid the foreclosure process.

Deed of Trust A provision that allows a lender to foreclose on a property in the event that the borrower defaults on the loan.

Default The state that occurs when a borrow fails to fulfill a duty or take care of an obligation, such as making monthly mortgage payments.

Deferred Maintenance Account A type of account that a borrower must fund to provide for maintenance of a property.

Deficiency Judgment The legal assignment of personal liability to a borrower for the unpaid balance of a mortgage, after foreclosing on the property has failed to yield the full amount of the debt.

Defined-Benefit Plan A type of benefit provided by an employer that defines an employee's benefits either as a fixed amount or a percentage of the beneficiary's salary when he retires.

Defined-Contribution Plan A type of benefit plan provided by an employer in which an employee's retirement benefits are determined by the amount that has been contributed by the employer and/or employee during the time of employment, and by the actual investment earnings on those contributions over the life of the fund.

Delinquency A state that occurs when the borrower fails to make mortgage payments on time, eventually resulting in foreclosure, if severe enough.

Delinquent Mortgage A mortgage in which the borrower is behind on payments.

Demising Wall The physical partition between the spaces of two tenants or from the building's common areas.

Deposit Also referred to as "Earnest Money." The funds that the buyer provides when offering to purchase property.

Depreciation A decline in the value of property or an asset, often used as a tax deductible item.

Derivative Securities A type of securities that has been created from other financial instruments.

Design/Build An approach in which a single individual or business is responsible for both the design and construction.

Disclosure A written statement, presented to a potential buyer, that lists information relevant to a piece of property, whether positive or negative.

Discount Points Fees that a lender charges in order to provide a lower interest rate.

Discount Rate A figure used to translate present value from future payments or receipts.

Discretion The amount of authority an adviser or manager is granted for investing and managing a client's capital.

Distraint The act of seizing a tenant's personal property when the tenant is in default, based on the right the landlord has in satisfying the debt.

Diversification The act of spreading individual investments out to insulate a portfolio against the risk of reduced yield or capital loss.

Dividend Yield The percentage of a security's market price that represents the annual dividend rate.

Dividend Distributions of cash or stock that stockholders receive.

Dividend-Ex Date The initial date on which a person purchasing the stock can no longer receive the most recently announced dividend.

Document Needs List The list of documents a lender requires from a potential borrower who is submitting a loan application.

Documentation Preparation Fee A fee that lenders, brokers, and/or settlement agents charge for the preparation of the necessary closing documents.

Dollar Stop An agreed amount of taxes and operating expenses each tenant must pay out on a prorated basis.

Down Payment The variance between the purchase price and the portion that the mortgage lender financed.

DOWNREIT A structure of organization that makes it possible for REITs to purchase properties using partnership units.

Draw A payment from the construction loan proceeds made to contractors, subcontractors, home builders, or suppliers.

Due Diligence The activities of a prospective purchaser or mortgager of real property for the purpose of confirming that the property is as represented by the seller and is not subject to environmental or other problems.

Due on Sale Clause The standard mortage language that states the loan must still be repaid if the property is resold.

Earnest Money See: Deposit.

Earthquake Insurance A type of insurance policy that provides coverage against earthquake damage to a home.

Easement The right given to a non-ownership party to use a certain part of the property for specified purposes, such as servicing power lines or cable lines.

Economic Feasibility The viability of a building or project in terms of costs and revenue where the degree of viability is established by extra revenue.

Economic Rent The market rental value of a property at a particular point in time.

Effective Age An estimate of the physical condition of a building presented by an appraiser.

Effective Date The date on which the sale of securities can commence once a registration statement becomes effective.

Effective Gross Income (EGI)

The total property income which rents and other sources generate after subtracting a vacancy factor estimated to be appropriate for the property.

Effective Gross Rent (EGR) The net rent that is generated after adjusting for tenant improvements and other capital costs, lease commissions and other sales expenses.

Effective Rent The actual rental rate that the landlord achieves after deducting the concession value from the base rental rate a tenant pays.

Electronic Authentication A way of providing proof that a particular electronic document is genuine, has arrived unaltered, and came from the indicated source.

Eminent Domain The power of the governement to pay the fair market value for a property, appropriating it for public use.

Encroachment Any improvement or upgrade that illegally intrudes onto another party's property.

Encumbrance Any right or interest in a property that interferes with using it or transfering ownership.

End Loan The result of converting to permanent financing from a construction loan.

Entitlement A benefit of a VA home loan. Often referred to as eligibility.

Environmental Impact Statement Legally required documents that must accompany major project proposals where there will likely be an impact on the surrounding environment.

Equal Credit Opportunity Act (ECOA) A federal law that requires a lender or other creditor to make credit available for applicants regardless of sex, marital status, race, religion, or age.

Equifax One of the three primary credit-reporting bureaus.

Equity The value of a property after existing liabilities have been deducted.

Employee Retirement Income Security Act (ERISA) A legislation that controls the investment activities, mainly of corporate and union pension plans.

Errors and Omissions Insurance A type of policy that insures against the mistakes of a builder or architect.

Escalation Clause The clause in a lease that provides for the rent to be increased to account for increases in the expenses the landlord must pay.

Escrow A valuable item, money or documents deposited with a third party for delivery upon the fulfillment of a condition.

Escrow Account Also referred to as an Impound Account. An account established by a mortgage lender or servicing company for the purpose of holding funds for the payment of items, such as homeowners insurance and property taxes.

Escrow Agent A neutral third party who makes sure that all conditions of a real estate transaction have been met

before any funds are transfered or property is recorded.

Escrow Agreement A written agreement between an escrow agent and the contractual parties which defines the basic obligations of each party, the money (or other valuables) to be deposited in escrow, and how the escrow agent is to dispose of the money on deposit.

Escrow Analysis An annual investigation a lender performs to make sure they are collecting the appropriate amount of money for anticipated expenditures.

Escrow Closing The event in which all conditions of a real estate transaction have been met, and the property title is transferred to the buyer.

Escrow Company A neutral company that serves as a third party to ensure that all conditions of a real estate transaction are met.

Escrow Disbursements The dispensing of escrow funds for the payment of real estate taxes, hazard insurance, mortgage insurance, and other property expenses as they are due.

Escrow Payment The funds that are withdrawn by a mortgage servicer from a borrower's escrow account to pay property taxes and insurance.

Estate The total assets, including property, of an individual after he has died.

Estimated Closing Costs An estimation of the expenses relating to the sale of real estate.

Estimated Hazard Insurance An estimation of hazard insurance, or homeowners' insurance, that will cover physical risks.

Estimated Property Taxes An estimation of the property taxes that must be paid on the property, according to state and county tax rates.

Estoppel Certificate A signed statement that certifies that certain factual statements are correct as of the date of the statement and can be relied upon by a third party, such as a prospective lender or purchaser.

Eviction The legal removal of an occupant from a piece of property.

Examination of Title A title company's inspection and report of public records and other documents for the purpose of determining the chain of ownership of a property.

Exclusive Agency Listing A written agreement between a property owner and a real estate broker in which the owner promises to pay the broker a commission if certain property is leased during the listing period.

Exclusive Listing A contract that allows a licensed real estate agent to be the only agent who can sell a property for a given time.

Executed Contract An agreement in which all parties involved have fulfilled their duties.

Executor The individual who is named in a will to administer an estate. Executrix is the feminine form.

Exit strategy An approach investors may use when they wish to liquidate all or part of their investment.

Experian One of the three primary credit-reporting bureaus.

Face Rental Rate The rental rate that the landlord publishes.

Facility Space The floor area in a hospitality property that is dedicated to activities, such as restaurants, health clubs, and gift shops that interactively service multiple people and is not directly related to room occupancy.

Funds Available for Distribution (FAD) The income from operations, with cash expenditures subtracted, that may be used for leasing commissions and tenant improvement costs.

FAD Multiple The price per share of a REIT divided by its funds available for distribution.

Fair Credit Reporting Act (FCRA) The federal legislation that governs the processes

credit reporting agencies must follow.

Fair Housing Act The federal legislation that prohibits the refusal to rent or sell to anyone based on race, color, religion, sex, family status, B268, or disability.

Fair Market Value The highest price that a buyer would be willing to pay, and the lowest a seller would be willing to accept.

Fannie Mae See: Federal National Mortgage Association.

Fannie Mae's Community Home Buyer's Program A community lending model based on borrower income in which mortgage insurers and Fannie Mae offer flexible underwriting guidelines in order to increase the buying power for a low- or moderate-income family and to decrease the total amount of cash needed to purchase a home.

Farmer's Home Administration (FMHA) An agency within the U.S. Department of Agriculture that provides credit to farmers and other rural residents.

Federal Home Loan Mortgage Corporation (FHLMC) Also known as Freddie Mac. The company that buys mortgages from lending institutions, combines them with other loans, and sells shares to investors.

Federal Housing Administration (FHA) A government agency that provides low-rate mortgages to buyers who are able to make a down payment as low as three percent.

Federal National Mortgage Association (FNMA) Also known as Fannie Mae. A congressionally chartered, shareholder-owned company that is the nation's largest supplier of home mortgage funds. The company buys mortgages from lenders and resells them as securities on the secondary mortgage market.

Fee Simple The highest possible interest a person can have in a piece of real estate.

Fee Simple Estate An unconditional, unlimited

inheritance estate in which the owner may dispose of or use the property as desired.

Fee Simple Interest The state of owning all the rights in a real estate parcel.

Funds From Operations (FFO) A ratio that is meant to highlight the amount of cash a company's real estate portfolio generates relative to its total operating cash flow.

FFO Multiple The price of a REIT share divided by its funds from operations.

FHA Loans Mortgages that the Federal Housing Administration (FHA) insures.

FHA Mortgage Insurance A type of insurance that requires a fee to be paid at closing in order to insure the loan with the Federal Housing Administration (FHA).

Fiduciary Any individual who holds authority over a plan's asset management, administration or disposition, or renders paid investment advice regarding a plan's assets.

Finance Charge The amount of interest to be paid on a loan or credit card balance.

Firm Commitment A written agreement a lender makes to loan money for the purchase of property.

First Mortgage The main mortgage on a property.

First Refusal Right/ Right of First Refusal A lease clause that gives a tenant the first opportunity to buy a property or to lease additional space in a property at the same price and terms as those contained in an offer from a third-party that the owner has expressed a willingness to accept.

First-Generation Space A new space that has never before been occupied by a tenant and is currently available for lease.

First-Loss Position A security's position that will suffer the first economic loss if the assets below it lose value or are foreclosed on.

Fixed Costs Expenses remain the same despite the level of sales or production.

Fixed Rate An interest rate that does not change over the life of the loan.

Fixed Time The particular weeks of a year that the owner of a timeshare arrangement can access his accommodations.

Fixed-Rate Mortgage A loan with an unchanging interest rate over the life of the loan.

Fixture Items that become a part of the property when they are permanently attached to the property.

Flat Fee An amount of money that an adviser or manager receives for managing a portfolio of real estate assets.

Flex Space A building that provides a flexible configuration of office or showroom space combined with manufacturing, laboratory, warehouse, distribution, etc.

Float The number of freely traded shares owned by the public.

Flood Certification The process of analyzing whether a property is located in a known flood zone.

Flood Insurance A policy that is required in designated flood zones to protect against loss due to flood damage.

Floor Area Ratio (FAR) A measurement of a building's gross square footage compared to the square footage of the land on which it is located.

For Sale By Owner (FSBO) A method of selling property in which the property owner serves as the selling agent and directly handles the sales process with the buyer or buyer's agent.

Force Majeure An external force that is not controlled by the contractual parties and prevents them from complying with the provisions of the contract.

Foreclosure The legal process in which a lender takes over ownership of a property once the borrower is in default in a mortgage arrangement.

Forward Commitments Contractual agreements to perform certain financing duties according to any stated conditions.

Four Quadrants of the Real Estate Capital Markets The four market types that consist of Private Equity, Public Equity, Private Debt, and Public Debt.

Freddie Mac See: Federal Home Loan Mortgage Corporation.

Front-End Ratio The measurement a lender uses to compare a borrower's monthly housing expense to gross monthly income.

Full Recourse A loan on which the responsibility of a loan is transferred to an endorser or guarantor in the event of default by the borrower.

Full-Service Rent A rental rate that includes all operating expenses and real estate taxes for the first year.

Fully Amortized ARM An ARM with a monthly payment that is sufficient to amortize the remaining balance at the current interest accrual rate over the amortization term.

Fully Diluted Shares The number of outstanding common stock shares if all convertible securities were converted to common shares.

Future Proposed Space The space in a commercial development that has been proposed but is not yet under construction, or the future phases of a multi-phase project that has not yet been built.

General Contractor The main person or business that contracts for the construction of an entire building or project, rather than individual duties.

General Partner The member in a partnership who holds the authority to bind the partnership and shares in its profits and losses.

Gift Money a buyer has received from a relative or other source.

Ginnie Mae See: Government National Mortgage Association.

Going-In Capitalization Rate The rate that is computed by dividing the expected net operating income for the first year by the value of the property.

Good Faith Estimate A lender's or broker's estimate that shows all costs associated with obtaining a home loan including loan processing, title, and inspection fees.

Government Loan A mortgage that is insured or guaranteed by the FHA, the Department of Veterans Affairs (VA), or the Rural Housing Service (RHS).

Government National Mortgage Association (GNMA) Also known as Ginnie Mae. A government-owned corporation under the U.S. Department of Housing and Urban Development (HUD) which performs the same role as Fannie Mae and Freddie Mac in providing funds to lenders for making home loans, but only purchases loans that are backed by the federal government.

Grace Period A defined time period in which a borrower may make a loan payment after its due date without incurring a penalty.

Graduated Lease A lease, usually long-term, in which rent payments vary in accordance with future contingencies.

Graduated Payment Mortgage
A mortgage that requires low payments during the first years of the loan, but eventually requires larger monthly payments over the term of the loan that become fixed later in the term.

Grant To give or transfer an interest in a property by deed or other documented method.

Grantee The party to whom an interest in a property is given.

Grantor The party who is transferring an interest in a property.

Gross Building Area The sum of areas at all floor levels, including the basement, mezzanine, and penthouses included in the principal outside faces of the exterior walls without allowing for architectural setbacks or projections.

Gross Income The total income of a household before taxes or expenses have been subtracted.

Gross Investment in Real Estate (Historic Cost) The total amount of equity and debt that is invested in a piece of real estate minus proceeds from sales or partial sales.

Gross Leasable Area The amount of floor space that is designed for tenants' occupancy and exclusive use.

Gross Lease A rental arrangement in which the tenant pays a flat sum for rent, and the landlord must pay all building expenses out of that amount.

Gross Real Estate Asset Value The total market value of the real estate investments under management in a fund or individual accounts, usually including the total value of all equity positions, debt positions, and joint venture ownership positions.

Gross Real Estate Investment Value The market value of real estate investments that are held in a portfolio without including debt.

Gross Returns The investment returns generated from

operating a property without adjusting for adviser or manager fees.

Ground Rent A long-term lease (e.g. 99 years) in which rent is paid to the land owner, normally to build something on that land.

Growing-Equity Mortgage A fixed-rate mortgage in which payments increase over a specified amount of time with the extra funds being applied to the principal.

Guarantor The part who makes a guaranty.

Guaranty An agreement in which the guarantor promises to satisfy the debt or obligations of another, if and when the debtor fails to do so.

Hard Cost The expenses attributes to actually constructing property improvements.

Hazard Insurance Also known as Homeowners' Insurance or Fire Insurance. A policy that provides coverage for damage from forces, such as fire and wind.

Highest and Best Use The most reasonable, expected, legal use of a piece of vacant land or improved property that is physically possible, supported appropriately, financially feasible, and that results in the highest value.

High-Rise In a suburban district, any building taller than six stories. In a business district, any building taller than 25 stories.

Holdbacks A portion of a loan funding that is not dispersed until an additional condition is met, such as the completion of construction.

Holding Period The expected length of time, from purchase to sale, that an investor will own a property.

Hold-Over Tenant A tenant who retains possession of the leased premises after the lease has expired.

Home Equity Conversion Mortgage (HECM) Also referred to as a Reverse Annuity Mortgage. A type of mortgage in which the lender makes payments to the owner, thereby enabling older homeowners to convert equity in their homes into cash in the form of monthly payments.

Home Equity Line An open-ended amount of credit based on the equity a homeowner has accumulated.

Home Equity Loan A type of loan that allows owners to borrow against the equity in their homes up to a limited amount.

Home Inspection A pre-purchase examination of the condition a home is in by a certified inspector.

Home Inspector A certified professional who determines the structural soundness and operating systems of a property.

Home Price The price that a buyer and seller agree upon, generally based on the home's appraised market value.

Homeowners' Association (HOA) A group that governs a community, condominium building, or neighborhood and enforces the covenants, conditions, and restrictions set by the developer.

Homeowners' Association Dues The monthly payments that are paid to the homeowners' association for maintenance and communal expenses.

Homeowners' Insurance A policy that includes coverage for all damages that may affect the value of a house as defined in the terms of the insurance policy.

Homeowner's Warranty A type of policy homebuyers often purchase to cover repairs, such as heating or air conditioning, should they stop working within the coverage period.

Homestead The property an owner uses as his primary residence.

Housing Expense Ratio The percentage of gross income that is devoted to housing costs each month.

HUD Housing and Urban Development. A federal agency that oversees a variety of housing and community development programs, including the FHA.

HUD Median Income The average income for families in a particular area, which is estimated by HUD.

HUD-1 Settlement Statement Also known as the Closing Statement or Settlement Sheet. An itemized listing of the funds paid at closing.

HUD-1 Uniform Settlement Statement A closing statement for the buyer and seller that describes all closing costs for a real estate transaction or refinancing.

HVAC Heating, Ventilating, and Air Conditioning.

Hybrid Debt A position in a mortgage that has equity-like features of participation in both cash flow and the appreciation of the property at the point of sale or refinance.

Implied Cap Rate The net operating income divided by the sum of a REIT's equity market capitalization and its total outstanding debt.

Impounds The part of the monthly mortgage payment that is reserved in an account in order to pay for hazard insurance, property taxes, and private mortgage insurance.

Improvements The upgrades or changes made to a building to improve its value or usefulness.

Incentive Fee A structure in which the fee amount charged is based on the performance of the real estate assets under management.

Income Capitalization Value The figure derived for an income-producing property by converting its expected benefits into property value.

Income Property A particular property that is used to generate income but is not occupied by the owner.

Income Return The percentage of the total return generated by the income from property, fund, or account operations.

Index A financial table that lenders use for calculating interest rates on ARMs.

Indexed Rate The sum of the published index with a margin added.

Indirect Costs Expenses of development other than the costs of direct material and labor that are related directly to the construction of improvements.

Individual Account Management The process of maintaining accounts that have been established for individual plan sponsors or other investors for investment in real estate, where a firm acts as an adviser in obtaining and/or managing a real estate portfolio.

Inflation Hedge An investment whose value tends to increase at a greater rate than inflation, contributing to the preservation of the purchasing power of a portfolio.

Inflation The rate at which consumer prices increase each year.

Initial Interest Rate The original interest rate on an ARM which is sometimes subject to a variety of adjustments throughout the mortgage.

Initial Public Offering (IPO) The first time a previously private company offers securities for public sale.

Initial Rate Cap The limit specified by some ARMs as the maximum amount the interest rate may increase when the initial interest rate expires.

Initial Rate Duration The date specified by most ARMs at which the initial rate expires.

Inspection Fee The fee that a licensed property inspector charges for determining the current physical condition of the property.

Inspection Report A written report of the property's condition presented by a licensed inspection professional.

Institutional-Grade Property A variety of types of real estate properties usually owned or financed by tax-exempt institutional investors.

Insurance Binder A temporary insurance policy that is implemented while a permanent policy is drawn up or obtained.

Insurance Company Separate Account A real estate investment vehicle only offered by life insurance companies, which enables an ERISA-governed fund to avoid creating unrelated taxable income for certain types of property investments and investment structures.

Insured Mortgage A mortgage that is guaranteed by the FHA or by private mortgage insurance (PMI).

Interest Accrual Rate The rate at which a mortgage accrues interest.

Interest Only Loan A mortgage for which the borrower pays only the interest that accrues on the loan balance each month.

Interest Paid over Life of Loan The total amount that has been paid to the lender during the time the money was borrowed.

Interest Rate The percentage that is charged for a loan.

Interest Rate Buy-Down Plans A plan in which a seller uses funds from the sale of the home to buy down the interest rate and reduce the buyer's monthly payments.

Interest Rate Cap The highest interest rate charge allowed on the monthly payment of an ARM during an adjustment period.

Interest rate ceiling The maximum interest rate a lender can charge for an ARM.

Interest Rate Floor The minimum possible interest rate a lender can charge for an ARM.

Interest The price that is paid for the use of capital.

Interest-Only Strip A derivative security that consists of all or part of the portion of interest in the underlying loan or security.

Interim Financing Also known as Bridge or Swing Loans. Short-term financing a seller uses to bridge the gap between the sale of one house and the purchase of another.

Internal Rate of Return (IRR) The calculation of a discounted cash-flow analysis which is used to determine the potential total return of a real estate asset during a particular holding period.

Inventory The entire space of a certain proscribed market without concern for its availability or condition.

Investment Committee The governing body that is charged with overseeing corporate pension investments and developing investment policies for board approval.

Investment Manager An individual or company that assumes authority over a specified amount of real estate capital, invests that capital in assets using a separate account, and provides asset management.

Investment Policy A document that formalizes an institution's goals, objectives, and guidelines for asset management, investment advisory contracting, fees, and utilization of consultants and other outside professionals.

Investment Property A piece of real estate that generates some form of income.

Investment Strategy The methods used by a manager in structuring a portfolio and selecting the real estate assets for a fund or an account.

Investment Structures Approaches to investing that include unleveraged acquisitions, leveraged acquisitions, traditional debt, participating debt, convertible debt, triple-net leases, and joint ventures.

Investment-Grade CMBS Commercial Mortgage-Backed Securities that have ratings of AAA, AA, A, or BBB.

Investor Status The position an investor is in, either taxable or tax-exempt.

Joint Liability The condition in which responsibility rests with two or more people for fulfilling the terms of a home loan or other financial debt.

Joint Tenancy A form of ownership in which two or more people have equal shares in a piece of property, and rights pass to the surviving owner(s) in the event of death.

Joint Venture An investment business formed by more than one party for the purpose of acquiring or developing and managing property and/or other assets.

Judgment The decision a court of law makes.

Judicial Foreclosure The usual foreclosure proceeding some states use, which is handled in a civil lawsuit.

Jumbo Loan A type of mortgage that exceeds the required limits set by Fannie Mae and Freddie Mac each year.

Junior Mortgage A loan that is a lower priority behind the primary loan.

Just Compensation The amount that is fair to both the owner and the government when property is appropriated for public use through Eminent Domain.

Landlord's Warrant The warrant a landlord obtains

to take a tenant's personal property to sell at a public sale to compel payment of the rent or other stipulation in the lease.

Late Charge The fee that is imposed by a lender when the borrower has not made a payment when it was due.

Late Payment The payment made to the lender after the due date has passed.

Lead Manager The investment banking firm that has primary responsibility for coordinating the new issuance of securities.

Lease A contract between a property owner and tenant that defines payments and conditions under which the tenant may occupy the real estate for a given period of time.

Lease Commencement Date The date at which the terms of the lease are implemented.

Lease Expiration Exposure Schedule A chart of the total square footage of all current leases that expire in each of the next five years, without taking renewal options into account.

Lease Option A financing option that provides for homebuyers to lease a home with an option to buy, with part of the rental payments being applied toward the down payment.

Leasehold The limited right to inhabit a piece of real estate held by a tenant.

Leasehold State A way of holding a property title in which the mortgagor does not actually own the property but has a long-term lease on it.

Leasehold Interest The right to hold or use property for a specific period of time at a given price without transfering ownership.

Lease-Purchase A contract that defines the closing date and solutions for the seller in the event that the buyer defaults.

Legal Blemish A negative count against a piece of property such as a zoning violation or fraudulent title claim.

Legal Description A way of describing and locating a piece

of real estate that is recognized by law.

Legal Owner The party who holds the title to the property, although the title may carry no actual rights to the property other than as a lien.

Lender A bank or other financial institution that offers home loans.

Letter of Credit A promise from a bank or other party that the issuer will honor drafts or other requests for payment upon complying with the requirements specified in the letter of credit.

Letter of Intent An initial agreement defining the proposed terms for the end contract.

Leverage The process of increasing the return on an investment by borrowing some of the funds at an interest rate less than the return on the project.

Liabilities A borrower's debts and financial obligations, whether long- or short-term.

Liability Insurance A type

of policy that protects owners against negligence, personal injury, or property damage claims.

LIBOR Acronym for "London Interbank Offered Rate." An index used to determine interest rate changes for adjustable rate mortgages. Very popular index for interest-only mortgage programs.

London InterBank Offered Rate (LIBOR) The interest rate offered on Eurodollar deposits traded between banks and used to determine changes in interest rate for ARMs.

Lien A claim put by one party on the property of another as collateral for money owed.

Lien Waiver A waiver of a mechanic's lien rights that is sometimes required before the general contractor can receive money under the payment provisions of a construction loan and contract.

Life Cap A limit on the amount an ARM's interest rate can increase during the mortgage term.

Lifecycle The stages of development for a property: pre-development, development, leasing, operating, and rehabilitation.

Lifetime Payment Cap A limit on the amount that payments can increase or decrease over the life of an ARM.

Lifetime Rate Cap The highest possible interest rate that may be charged, under any circumstances, over the entire life of an ARM.

Like-Kind Property A term that refers to real estate that is held for productive use in a trade or business or for investment.

Limited Partnership A type of partnership in which some partners manage the business and are personally liable for partnership debts, but some partners contribute capital and share in profits without the responsibility of management.

Line of Credit An amount of credit granted by a financial institution up to a specified amount for a certain period of time to a borrower.

Liquid Asset A type of asset that can be easily converted into cash.

Liquidity The ease with which an individual's or company's assets can be converted to cash without losing their value.

Listing Agreement An agreement between a property owner and a real estate broker which authorizes the broker to attempt to sell or lease the property at a specified price and terms in return for a commission or other compensation.

Loan An amount of money that is borrowed and usually repaid with interest.

Loan Application A document that presents a borrower's income, debt, and other obligations to determine credit worthiness, as well as some basic information on the target property.

Loan Application Fee A fee lenders charge to cover expenses relating to reviewing a loan application.

Loan Commitment An agreement by a lender or other financial institution to make or insure a loan for the specified amount and terms.

Loan Officer An official representative of a lending institution who is authorized to act on behalf of the lender within specified limits.

Loan Origination The process of obtaining and arranging new loans.

Loan Origination Fee A fee lenders charge to cover the costs related to arranging the loan.

Loan Servicing The process a lending institution goes through for all loans it manages. This involves processing payments, sending statements, managing the escrow/impound account, providing collection services on delinquent loans, ensuring that insurance and property taxes are made on the property, handling pay-offs and assumptions, as well as various other services.

Loan Term The time, usually expressed in years, that a lender sets in which a buyer must pay a mortgage.

Loan-to-Value (LTV) The ratio of the amount of the loan compared to the appraised value or sales price.

Lock-Box Structure An arrangement in which the payments are sent directly from the tenant or borrower to the trustee.

Lock-In A commitment from a lender to a borrower to guarantee a given interest rate for a limited amount of time.

Lock-In Period The period of time during which the borrower is guaranteed a specified interest rate.

Lockout The period of time during which a loan may not be paid off early.

Long-Term Lease A rental agreement that will last at least three years from initial signing to the date of expiration or renewal.

Loss Severity The percentage of lost principal when a loan is foreclosed.

Lot One of several contiguous parcels of a larger piece of land.

Low-Documentation Loan A mortage that requires only a basic verification of income and assets.

Low-Rise A building that involves fewer than four stories above the ground level.

Lump-Sum Contract A type of construction contract that requires the general contractor to complete a building project for a fixed cost that is usually established beforehand by competitive bidding.

Magic Page A story of projected growth which describes how a new REIT will achieve its future plans for funds from operations or funds available for distribution.

Maintenance Fee The charge to homeowners' association members each month for the repair and maintenance of common areas.

Maker One who issues a promissory note and commits to paying the note when it is due.

Margin A percentage that is added to the index and fixed for the mortgage term.

Mark to Market The act of changing the original investment cost or value of a property or portfolio to the level of the current estimated market value.

Market Capitalization A measurement of a company's value that is calculated by multiplying the current share price by the current number of shares outstanding.

Market Rental Rates The rental income that a landlord could most likely ask for a property in the open market, indicated by the current rents for comparable spaces.

Market Study A forecast of the demand for a certain type of real estate project in the future which includes an estimate of the square footage that could be absorbed and the rents that could be charged.

Market Value The price a property would sell for at a particular point in time in a competitive market.

Marketable Title A title that is free of encumbrances and can be marketed immediately to a willing purchaser.

Master Lease The primary lease that controls other subsequent leases and may cover more property than all subsequent leases combined.

Master Servicer An entity that acts on behalf of a trustee for security holders' benefit in collecting funds from a borrower, advancing funds in the event of delinquencies and, in the event of default, taking a property through foreclosure.

Maturity Date The date at which the total principal balance of a loan is due.

Mechanic's Lien A claim created for securing payment priority for the price and value of work performed and materials furnished in constructing, repairing, or improving a building or other structure.

Meeting Space The space in hotels that is made available to the public to rent for meetings, conferences, or banquets.

Merged Credit Report A report that combines information from the three primary credit-reporting agencies including: Equifax, Experian, and Trans Union.

Metes and Bounds The surveyed boundary lines of a piece of land described by listing the compass directions (bounds) and distances (metes) of the boundaries.

Mezzanine Financing A financing position somewhere between equity and debt, meaning that there are higher-priority debts above and equity below.

Mid-Rise Usually, a building which shows four to eight stories above ground level. In a business district, buildings up to 25 stories may also be included.

Mixed-Use A term referring to space within a building or project which can be used for more than one activity.

Modern Portfolio Theory (MPT) An approach of quantifying risk and return in an asset portfolio which emphasizes the portfolio rather than the individual assets and how the assets perform in relation to each other.

Modification An adjustment in the terms of a loan agreement.

Modified Annual Percentage Rate (APR) An index of the cost of a loan based on the standard APR but adjusted for the amount of time the borrower expects to hold the loan.

Monthly Association Dues A payment due each month to a homeowners' association for expenses relating to maintenance and community operations.

Mortgage An amount of money that is borrowed to purchase a property using that property as collateral.

Mortgage Acceleration Clause A provision enabling a lender to require that the rest of the loan balance is paid in a lump sum under certain circumstances.

Mortgage Banker A financial

institution that provides home loans using its own resources, often selling them to investors such as insurance companies or Fannie Mae.

Mortgage Broker An individual that matches prospective borrowers with lenders that the broker is approved to deal with.

Mortgage Broker Business A company that matches prospective borrowers with lenders that the broker is approved to deal with.

Mortgage Constant A figure comparing an amortizing mortgage payment to the outstanding mortgage balance.

Mortgage Insurance (MI) A policy, required by lenders on some loans, that covers the lender against certain losses that are incurred as a result of a default on a home loan.

Mortgage Insurance Premium (MIP) The amount charged for mortgage insurance, either to a government agency or to a private MI company.

Mortgage Interest Deduction
The tax write-off that the IRS allows most homeowners to deduct for annual interest payments made on real estate loans.

Mortgage Life and Disability Insurance A type of term life insurance borrowers often purchase to cover debt that is left when the borrower dies or becomes too disabled to make the mortgage payments.

Mortgagee The financial institution that lends money to the borrower.

Mortgagor The person who requests to borrow money to purchase a property.

Multidwelling Units A set of properties that provide separate housing areas for more than one family but only require a single mortgage.

National Association of Real Estate Investment Trusts (NAREIT) The national, non-profit trade organization that represents the real estate investment trust industry.

National Council of Real Estate Investment Fiduciaries

(NCREIF) A group of real estate professionals who serve on committees, sponsor research articles, seminars and symposiums, and produce the NCREIF Property Index.

NCREIF Property Index (NPI) A quarterly and yearly report presenting income and appreciation components.

Negative Amortization An event that occurs when the deferred interest on an ARM is added, and the balance increases instead of decreases.

Net Asset Value (NAV) The total value of an asset or property minus leveraging or joint venture interests.

Net Asset Value Per Share The total value of a REIT's current assets divided by outstanding shares.

Net Assets The total value of assets minus total liabilities based on market value.

Net Cash Flow The total income generated by an investment property after expenses have been subtracted.

Net Investment in Real Estate Gross investment in properties minus the outstanding balance of debt.

Net Investment Income The income or loss of a portfolio or business minus all expenses, including portfolio and asset management fees, but before gains and losses on investments are considered.

Net Operating Income (NOI) The pre-tax figure of gross revenue minus operating expenses and an allowance for expected vacancy.

Net Present Value (NPV) The sum of the total current value of incremental future cash flows plus the current value of estimated sales proceeds.

Net Purchase Price The gross purchase price minus any associated financed debt.

Net Real Estate Investment Value The total market value of all real estate minus property-level debt.

Net Returns The returns paid to investors minus fees to advisers or managers.

Net Sales Proceeds The income from the sale of an asset, or part of an asset, minus brokerage commissions, closing costs, and market expenses.

Net Square Footage The total space required for a task or staff position.

Net Worth The worth of an individual or company figured on the basis of a difference between all assets and liabilities.

No-Cash-Out Refinance Sometimes referred to as a Rate and Term Refinance. A refinancing transaction which is intended only to cover the balance due on the current loan and any costs associated with obtaining the new mortgage.

No-Cost Loan A loan for which there are no costs associated with the loan that are charged by the lender, but with a slightly higher interest rate.

No-Documentation Loan A type of loan application that requires no income or asset verification, usually granted based on strong credit with a large down payment.

Nominal Yield The yield investors receive before it is adjusted for fees, inflation, or risk.

Non-Assumption Clause A provision in a loan agreement that prohibits transfering a mortgage to another borrower without approval from the lender.

Non-Compete Clause A provision in a lease agreement that specifies that the tenant's business is the only one that may operate in the property in question, thereby preventing a competitor moving in next door.

Non-Conforming Loan Any loan that is too large or does not meet certain qualifications to be purchased by Fannie Mae or Freddie Mac.

Non-Discretionary Funds The funds that are allocated to an investment manager who must have approval from the investor for each transaction.

Non-Investment-Grade CMBS Also referred to as High-Yield CMBS. Commercial Mortgage-Backed Securities that have ratings of BB or B.

Non-Liquid Asset A type of asset that is not turned into cash very easily.

Non-Performing Loan A loan agreement that cannot meet its contractual principal and interest payments.

Non-Recourse Debt A loan that limits the lender's options to collect on the value of the real estate in the event of a default by the borrower.

Nonrecurring Closing Costs Fees that are only paid one time in a given transaction.

Note A legal document requiring a borrower to repay a mortgage at a specified interest rate over a certain period of time.

Note Rate The interest rate that is defined in a mortgage note.

Notice of Default A formal written notification a borrower receives once the borrower is in default stating that legal action may be taken.

Offer A term that describes a specified price or spread to sell whole loans or securities.

One-Year Adjustable Rate Mortgage An ARM for which the interest rate changes annually, generally based on movements of a published index plus a specified margin.

Open Space A section of land or water that has been dedicated for public or private use or enjoyment.

Open-End Fund A type of commingled fund with an infinite life, always accepting new investor capital and making new investments in property.

Operating Cost Escalation A clause that is intended to adjust rents to account for external standards such as published indexes, negotiated wage levels, or building-related expenses.

Operating Expense The regular costs associated with operating and managing a property.

Opportunistic A phrase that generally describes a strategy of holding investments in underperforming and/or undermanaged assets with the expectation of increases in cash flow and/or value.

Option A condition in which the buyer pays for the right to purchase a property within a certain period of time without the obligation to buy.

Option Arm Loan A type of mortgage in which the borrower has a variety of payment options each month.

Original Principal Balance The total principal owed on a mortgage before a borrower has made a payment.

Origination Fee A fee that most lenders charge for the purpose of covering the costs associated with arranging the loan.

Originator A company that underwrites loans for commercial and/or multi-family properties.

Out-Parcel The individual retail sites located within a shopping center.

Overallotment A practice in which the underwriters offer and sell a higher number of shares than they had planned to purchase from the issuer.

Owner Financing A transaction in which the property seller agrees to finance all or part of the amount of the purchase.

Parking Ratio A figure, generally expressed as square footage, that compares a building's total rentable square footage to its total number of parking spaces.

Partial Payment An amount paid that is not large enough to cover the normal monthly payment on a mortgage loan.

Partial Sales The act of selling a real estate interest that is smaller than the whole property.

Partial Taking The appropriating of a portion of an owner's property under the laws of eminent domain.

Participating Debt Financing that allows the lender to have participatory rights to equity through increased income and/or residual value over the balance of the loan or original value at the time the loan is funded.

Party in Interest Any party that may hold an interest, including employers, unions and, sometimes, fiduciaries.

Pass-Through Certificate A document that allows the holder to receive payments of principal and interest from the underlying pool of mortgages.

Payment Cap The maximum amount a monthly payment may increase on an ARM.

Payment Change Date The date on which a new payment amount takes effect on an ARM or GPM, usually in the month directly after the adjustment date.

Payout Ratio The percentage of the primary earnings per share, excluding unusual items, that are paid to common stockholders as cash dividends during the next 12 months.

Pension Liability The full amount of capital that is required to finance vested pension fund benefits.

Percentage Rent The amount of rent that is adjusted based on the percentage of gross sales or revenues the tenant receives.

Per-Diem Interest The interest that is charged or accrued daily.

Performance Bond A bond that contractor posts to guarantee full performance of a contract in which the proceeds will be used for completing the contract or compensating the owner for loss in the event of nonperformance.

Performance Measurement The process of measuring how well an investor's real estate has performed regarding individual assets, advisers/managers, and portfolios.

Performance The changes each quarter in fund or account values that can be explained by investment income, realized or unrealized appreciation, and the total return to the investors before and after investment management fees.

Performance-Based Fees The fees that advisers or managers receive which are based on returns to investors.

Periodic Payment Cap The highest amount that payments

can increase or decrease during a given adjustment period on an ARM.

Periodic Rate Cap The maximum amount that the interest rate can increase or decrease during a given adjustment period on an ARM.

Permanent Loan A long-term property mortgage.

Personal Property Any items belonging to a person that is not real estate.

PITI Principal, Interest, Taxes, Insurance. The items that are included in the monthly payment to the lender for an impounded loan, as well as mortgage insurance.

PITI Reserves The amount in cash that a borrower must readily have after the down payment and all closing costs are paid when purchasing a home.

Plan Assets The assets included in a pension plan.

Plan Sponsor The party that is responsible for administering an employee benefit plan.

Planned Unit Development (PUD) A type of ownership where individuals actually own the building or unit they live in, but common areas are owned jointly with the other members of the development or association. Contrast with condominium, where an individual actually owns the airspace of his unit, but the buildings and common areas are owned jointly with the others in the development or association.

Plat A chart or map of a certain area showing the boundaries of individual lots, streets, and easements.

Pledged Account Mortgage (PAM) A loan tied to a pledged savings account for which the fund and earned interest are used to gradually reduce mortgage payments.

Point Also referred to as a Discount Point. A fee a lender charges to provide a lower interest rate, equal to one percent of the amount of the loan.

Portfolio Management A process that involves

formulating, modifying, and implementing a real estate investment strategy according to an investor's investment objectives.

Portfolio Turnover The amount of time averaged from the time an investment is funded until it is repaid or sold.

Power of Attorney A legal document that gives someone the authority to act on behalf of another party.

Power of Sale The clause included in a mortgage or deed of trust that provides the mortgagee (or trustee) with the right and power to advertise and sell the property at public auction if the borrower is in default.

Pre-Approval The complete analysis a lender makes regarding a potential borrower's ability to pay for a home as well as a confirmation of the proposed amount to be borrowed.

Pre-Approval Letter The letter a lender presents which states the amount of money they are willing to lend a potential buyer.

Preferred Shares Certain stocks that have a prior distributions claim up to a defined amount before the common shareholders may receive anything.

Preleased A certain amount of space in a proposed building that must be leased before construction may begin or a certificate of occupancy may be issued.

Prepaid Expenses The amount of money that is paid before it is due, including including taxes, insurance, and/or assessments.

Prepaid Fees The charges that a borrower must pay in advance regarding certain recurring items, such as interest, property taxes, hazard insurance, and PMI, if applicable.

Prepaid Interest The amount of interest that is paid before its due date.

Prepayment The money that is paid to reduce the principal balance of a loan before the date it is due.

Prepayment Penalty A penalty that may be charged to the borrower when he pays off a loan before the planned maturity date.

Prepayment Rights The right a borrower is given to pay the total principal balance before the maturity date free of penalty.

Prequalification The initial assessment by a lender of a potential borrower's ability to pay for a home as well as an estimate of how much the lender is willing to supply to the buyer.

Price to Earnings Ratio The comparison that is derived by dividing the current share price by the sum of the primary earnings per share from continuing operations over the past year.

Primary Issuance The preliminary financing of an issuer.

Prime Rate The best interest rate reserved for a bank's preferred customers.

Prime Space The first-generation space that is available for lease.

Prime Tenant The largest or highest-earning tenant in a building or shopping center.

Principal The amount of money originally borrowed in a mortgage, before interest is included and with any payments subtracted.

Principal Balance The total current balance of mortgage principal not including interest.

Principal Paid over Life of Loan The final total of scheduled payments to the principal which the lender calculates to equal the face amount of the loan.

Principal Payments The lender's return of invested capital.

Principle of Conformity The concept that a property will probably increase in value if its size, age, condition, and style are similar to other properties in the immediate area.

Private Debt Mortgages or other liabilities for which an individual is responsible.

Private Equity A real estate investment that has been acquired by a noncommercial entity.

Private Mortgage Insurance (PMI) A type of policy that a lender requires when the borrower's down payment or home equity percentage is under 20 percent of the value of the property.

Private Placement The sale of a security in a way that renders it exempt from the registration rules and requirements of the SEC.

Private REIT A real estate investment company that is structured as a real estate investment trust and which places and holds shares privately rather than publicly.

Pro Rata The proportionate amount of expenses per tenant for the property's maintenance and operation.

Processing Fee A fee some lenders charge for gathering the information necessary to process the loan.

Production Acres The portion of land that can be used directly in agriculture or timber activities to generate income, but not areas used for such things as machinery storage or support.

Prohibited Transaction Certain transactions that may not be performed between a pension plan and a party in interest, such as the following: the sale, exchange or lease of any property; a loan or other grant of credit; and furnishing goods or services.

Promissory Note A written agreement to repay the specific amount over a certain period of time.

Property Tax The tax that must be paid on private property.

Prudent Man Rule The standard to which ERISA holds a fiduciary accountable.

Public Auction An annouced public meeting held at a specified location for the purpose of selling property to repay a mortgage in default.

Public Debt Mortgages or other liabilities for which

a commercial entity is responsible.

Public Equity A real estate investment that has been acquired by REITs and other publicly traded real estate operating companies.

Punch List An itemized list that documents incomplete or unsatisfactory items after the contractor has declared the space to be mostly complete.

Purchase Agreement The written contract the buyer and seller both sign defining the terms and conditions under which a property is sold.

Purchase Money Transaction A transaction in which property is acquired through the exchange of money or something of equivalent value.

Purchase-Money Mortgage (PMM) A mortgage obtained by a borrower which serves as partial payment for a property.

Qualified Plan Any employee benefit plan that the IRS has approved as a tax-exempt plan.

Qualifying Ratio The measurement a lender uses to determine how much they are willing to lend to a potential buyer.

Quitclaim Deed A written document that releases a party from any interest they may have in a property.

Rate Cap The highest interest rate allowed on a monthly payment during an adjustment period of an ARM.

Rate Lock The commitment of a lender to a borrower that guarantees a certain interest rate for a specific amount of time.

Rate-Improvement Mortgage A loan that includes a clause which entitles a borrower to a one-time-only cut in the interest rate without having to refinance.

Rating Agencies Independent firms that are engaged to rate securities' creditworthiness on behalf of investors.

Rating A figure that represents the credit quality or creditworthiness of securities.

Raw Land A piece of property that has not been developed and remains in its natural state.

Raw Space Shell space in a building that has not yet been developed.

Real Estate Agent An individual who is licensed to negotiate and transact the real estate sales.

Real Estate Fundamentals The factors that drive the value of property.

Real Estate Settlement Procedures Act (RESPA) A legislation for consumer protection that requires lenders to notify borrowers regarding closing costs in advance.

Real Property Land and anything else of a permanent nature that is affixed to the land.

Real Rate of Return The yield given to investors minus an inflationary factor.

Realtor A real estate agent or broker who is an active member of a local real estate board affiliated with the National Association of Realtors.

Recapture The act of the IRS recovering the tax benefit of a deduction or a credit that a taxpayer has previously taken in error.

Recorder A public official who records transactions that affect real estate in the area.

Recording The documentation that the registrar's office keeps of the details of properly executed legal documents.

Recording Fee A fee real estate agents charge for moving the sale of a piece of property into the public record.

Recourse The option a lender has for recovering losses against the personal assets of a secondary party who is also liable for a debt that is in default.

Red Herring An early prospectus that is distributed to prospective investors that includes a note in red ink on the cover stating that the SEC-approved registration statement is not yet in effect.

Refinance Transaction The act of paying off an existing loan using the funding gained from a new loan which uses the same property as security.

Regional Diversification Boundaries that are defined based on geography or economic lines.

Registration Statement The set of forms that are filed with the SEC (or the appropriate state agency) regarding a proposed offering of new securities or the listing of outstanding securities on a national exchange.

Regulation Z A federal legislation under the Truth in Lending Act that requires lenders to advise the borrower in writing of all costs that are associated with the credit portion of a financial transaction.

Rehab Short for Rehabilitation. Refers to an extensive renovation intended to extend the life of a building or project.

Rehabilitation Mortgage A loan meant to fund the repairing and improving of a resale home or building.

Real Estate Investment Trust (REIT) A trust corporation that combines the capital of several investors for the purpose of acquiring or providing funding for real estate.

Remaining Balance The amount of the principal on a home loan that has not yet been paid.

Remaining Term The original term of the loan after the number of payments made has been subtracted.

Real Estate Mortgage Investment Conduit (REMIC) An investment vehicle that is designed to hold a pool of mortgages solely to issue multiple classes of mortgage-backed securities in a way that avoids doubled corporate tax.

Renewal Option A clause in a lease agreement that allows a tenant to extend the term of a lease.

Renewal Probability The average percentage of a building's tenants who are expected to renew terms at market rental rates upon the lease expiration.

Rent Commencement Date
The date at which a tenant is to begin paying rent.

Rent Loss Insurance A policy that covers loss of rent or rental value for a landlord due to any condition that renders the leased premises inhabitable, thereby excusing the tenant from paying rent.

Rent The fee paid for the occupancy and/or use of any rental property or equipment.

Rentable/Usable Ratio A total rentable area in a building divided by the area available for use.

Rental Concession See: Concessions.

Rental Growth Rate The projected trend of market rental rates over a particular period of analysis.

Rent-Up Period The period of time following completion of a new building when tenants are actively being sought and the project is stabilizing.

Real Estate Owned (REO)
The real estate that a savings institution owns as a result of

foreclosure on borrowers in default.

Repayment Plan An agreement made to repay late installments or advances.

Replacement Cost The projected cost by current standards of constructing a building that is equivalent to the building being appraised.

Replacement Reserve Fund
Money that is set aside for replacing of common property in a condominium, PUD, or cooperative project.

Request for Proposal (RFP)
A formal request that invites investment managers to submit information regarding investment strategies, historical investment performance, current investment opportunities, investment management fees, and other pension fund client relationships used by their firm.

Rescission The legal withdrawing of a contract or consent from the parties involved.

Reserve Account An account

that must be funded by the borrower to protect the lender.

Resolution Trust Corp. (RTC) The congressional corporation established for the purpose of containing, managing, and selling failed financial institutions, thereby recovering taxpayer funds.

Retail Investor An investor who sells interests directly to consumers.

Retention Rate The percentage of trailing year's earnings that have been dispersed into the company again. It is calculated as 100 minus the trailing 12-month payout ratio.

Return on Assets The measurement of the ability to produce net profits efficiently by making use of assets.

Return on Equity The measurement of the return on the investment in a business or property.

Return on Investments The percentage of money that has been gained as a result of certain investments.

Reverse Mortgage See: Home Equity Conversion Mortgage.

Reversion Capitalization Rate The capitalization rate that is used to derive reversion value.

Reversion Value A benefit that an investor expects to receive as a lump sum at the end of an investment.

Revolving Debt A credit arrangement which enables a customer to borrow against a predetermined line of credit when purchasing goods and services.

Revenue Per Available Room (RevPAR) The total room revenue for a particular period divided by the average number of rooms available in a hospitality facility.

Right of Ingress or Egress The option to enter or to leave the premises in question.

Right of Survivorship The option that survivors have to take on the interest of a deceased joint tenant.

Right to Rescission A legal provision that enables borrowers to cancel certain loan types within three days after they sign.

Risk Management A logical approach to analyzing and defining insurable and non-insurable risks while evaluating the availability and costs of purchasing third-party insurance.

Risk-Adjusted Rate of Return A percentage that is used to identify investment options that are expected to deliver a positive premium despite their volatility.

Road Show A tour of the executives of a company that is planning to go public, during which the executives travel to a variety cities to make presentations to underwriters and analysts regarding their company and IPO.

Roll-Over Risk The possibility that tenants will not renew their lease.

Sale-Leaseback An arrangement in which a seller deeds a property, or part of it, to a buyer in exchange for money or the equivalent, then leases the property from the new owner.

Sales Comparison Value A value that is calculated by comparing the appraised property to similar properties in the area that have been recently sold.

Sales Contract An agreement that both the buyer and seller sign defining the terms of a property sale.

Second Mortgage A secondary loan obtained upon a piece of property.

Secondary Market A market in which existing mortgages are bought and sold as part of a mortgages pool.

Secondary (Follow-On) Offering An offering of stock made by a company that is already public.

Second-Generation or Secondary Space Space that has been occupied before and becomes available for lease again, either by the landlord or as a sublease.

Secured Loan A loan that is secured by some sort of collateral.

Securities and Exchange Commission (SEC) The federal agency that oversees the issuing and exchanging of public securities.

Securitization The act of converting a non-liquid asset into a tradable form.

Security The property or other asset that will serve as a loan's collateral.

Security Deposit An amount of money a tenant gives to a landlord to secure the performance of terms in a lease agreement.

Seisen (Seizen) The ownership of real property under a claim of freehold estate.

Self-Administered REIT A REIT in which the management are employees of the REIT or similar entity.

Self-Managed REIT See: Self-Administered REIT.

Seller Carry-Back An arrangement in which the seller provides the financing to purchase a home.

Seller Financing A type of funding in which the borrower may use part of the equity in the property to finance the purchase.

Senior Classes The security classes who have the highest priority for receiving payments from the underlying mortgage loans.

Separate Account A relationship in which a single pension plan sponsor is used to retain an investment manager or adviser under a stated investment policy exclusively for that sponsor.

Servicer An organization that collects principal and interest payments from borrowers and manages borrowers' escrow accounts on behalf of a trustee.

Servicing The process of collecting mortgage payments from borrowers as well as related responsibilities.

Setback The distance required from a given reference point before a structure can be built.

Settlement or Closing Fees Fees that the escrow agent

receives for carrying out the written instructions in the agreement between borrower and lender and/or buyer and seller.

Settlement Statement See: HUD-1 Settlement Statement.

Shared-Appreciation Mortgage A loan which enables a lender or other party to share in the profits of the borrower when the borrower sells the home.

Shared-Equity Transaction A transaction in which two people purchase a property, one as a residence and the other as an investment.

Shares Outstanding The number of shares of outstanding common stock minus the treasury shares.

Site Analysis A determination of how suitable a specific parcel of land is for a particular use.

Site Development The implementation of all improvements that are needed for a site before construction may begin.

Site Plan A detailed description and map of the location of improvements to a parcel.

Slab The flat, exposed surface that is laid over the structural support beams to form the building's floor(s).

Social Investing A strategy in which investments are driven in partially or completely by social or non-real estate objectives.

Soft Cost The part of an equity investment, aside from the literal cost of the improvements, that could be tax-deductible in the first year.

Space Plan A chart or map of space requirements for a tenant which include wall/door locations, room sizes, and even furniture layouts.

Special Assessment Certain charges that are levied against real estates for public improvements to benefit the property in question.

Special Servicer A company that is hired to collect on mortgages that are either delinquent or in default.

Specified Investing A strategy

of investment in individually specified properties, portfolios, or commingled funds are fully or partially detailed prior to the commitment of investor capital.

Speculative Space Any space in a rental property that has not been leased prior to construction on a new building begins.

Stabilized Net Operating Income Expected income minus expenses that reflect relatively stable operations.

Stabilized Occupancy The best projected range of long-term occupancy that a piece of rental property will achieve after existing in the open market for a reasonable period of time with terms and conditions that are comparable to similar offerings.

Step-Rate Mortgage A loan which allows for a gradual interest rate increase during the first few years of the loan.

Step-Up Lease (Graded Lease) A lease agreement which specifies certain increases in rent at certain intervals during the complete term of the lease.

Straight Lease (Flat Lease) A lease agreement which specifies an amount of rent that should be paid regularly during the complete term of the lease.

Strip Center Any shopping area that is made up of a row of stores but is not large enough to be anchored by a grocery store.

Subcontractor A contractor who has been hired by the general contractor, often specializing in a certain required task for the construction project.

Subdivision The most common type of housing development created by dividing a larger tract of land into individual lots for sale or lease.

Sublessee A person or business that holds the rights of use and occupancy under a lease contract with the original lessee, who still retains primary responsibility the lease obligations.

Subordinate Financing Any loan with a priority lower than loans that were obtained beforehand.

Subordinate Loan A second or third mortgage obtained with the same property being used as collateral.

Subordinated Classes Classes that have the lowest priority of receiving payments from underlying mortgage loans.

Subordination The act of sharing credit loss risk at varying rates among two or more classes of securities.

Subsequent Rate Adjustments The interest rate for ARMs that adjusts at regular intervals, sometimes differing from the duration period of the initial interest rate.

Subsequent Rate Cap The maximum amount the interest rate may increase at each regularly scheduled interest rate adjustment date on an ARM.

Super Jumbo Mortgage A loan that is over $650,000 for some lenders or $1,000,000 for others.

Surety A person who willingly binds himself to the debt or obligation of another party.

Surface Rights A right or easement that is usually granted with mineral rights which enabling the holder to drill through the surface.

Survey A document or analysis containing the precise measurements of a piece of property as performed by a licensed surveyor.

Sweat Equity The non-cash improvements in value that an owner adds to a piece of property.

Synthetic Lease A transaction that is considered to be a lease by accounting standards but a loan by tax standards.

Taking Similar to condemning, or any other interference with rights to private property, but a physical seizure or appropriation is not required.

Tax Base The determined value of all property that lies within the jurisdiction of the taxing authority.

Tax Lien A type of lien placed against a property if the owner has not paid property or personal taxes.

Tax Roll A record, that contains the descriptions of all land parcels and their owners, that is located within the county.

Tax Service Fee A fee that is charged for the purpose of setting up monitoring of the borrower's property tax payments by a third-party.

Teaser Rate A small, short-term interest rate offered on a mortgage in order to convince the potential borrower to apply.

Tenancy by the Entirety A form of ownership held by spouses in which they both hold title to the entire property with right of survivorship.

Tenancy in Common A type of ownership held by two or more owners in an undivided interest in the property with no right of survivorship.

Tenant (Lessee) A party who rents a piece of real estate from another by way of a lease agreement.

Tenant at Will A person who possesses a piece of real estate with the owner's permission.

Tenant Improvement (TI) Allowance The specified amount of money that the landlord contributes toward tenant improvements.

Tenant Improvement (TI) The upgrades or repairs that are made to the leased premises by or for a tenant.

Tenant Mix The quality of the income stream for a property.

Term The length that a loan lasts or is expected to last before it is repaid.

Third-Party Origination A process in which another party is used by the lender to originate, process, underwrite, close, fund, or package the mortgages it expects to deliver to the secondary mortgage market.

Timeshare A form of ownership involving purchasing a specific period of time or percentage of interest in a vacation property.

Time-Weighted Average Annual Rate of Return The regular yearly return over several years that would have the same return value as combining the actual annual returns for each year in the series.

Title The legal written document which provides someone ownership in a piece of real estate.

Title Company A business that determines that a property title is clear and that provides title insurance.

Title Exam An analysis of the public records in order to confirm that the seller is the legal owner, and there are no encumbrances on the property.

Title Insurance A type of policy that is issued to both lenders and buyers to cover loss due to property ownership disputes that may arise at a later date.

Title Insurance Binder A written promise from the title insurance company to insure the title to the property, based on the conditions and exclusions shown in the binder.

Title Risk The potential impediments in transfering a title from one party to another.

Title Search The process of analyzing all transactions existing in the public record in order to determine whether any title defects could interfere with the clear transfer of property ownership.

Total Acres The complete amount of land area that is contained within a real estate investment.

Total Assets The final amount of all gross investments, cash and equivalents, receivables, and other assets as they are presented on the balance sheet.

Total Commitment The complete funding amount that is promised once all specified conditions have been met.

Total Expense Ratio The comparison of monthly debt obligations to gross monthly income.

Total Inventory The total amount of square footage commanded by property within a geographical area.

Total Lender Fees Charges which the lender requires for obtaining the loan, aside from other fees associated with the transfer of a property.

Total Loan Amount The basic amount of the loan plus any additional financed closing costs.

Total Monthly Housing Costs The amount that must be paid each month to cover principal, interest, property taxes, PMI, and/or either hazard insurance or homeowners' association dues.

Total of All Payments The total cost of the loan after figuring the sum of all monthly interest payments.

Total Principal Balance The sum of all debt, including the original loan amount adjusted for subsequent payments and any unpaid items that may be included in the principal balance by the mortgage note or by law.

Total Retail Area The total floor area of a retail center that is currently leased or available for lease.

Total Return The final amount of income and appreciation returns per quarter.

Townhouse An attached home that is not considered to be a condominium.

Trade Fixtures Any personal property that is attached to a structure and used in the business but is removable once the lease is terminated.

Trading Down The act of purchasing a property that is less expensive than the one currently owned.

Trading Up The act of purchasing a property that is more expensive than the one currently owned.

Tranche A class of securities that may or may not be rated.

Trans Union Corporation One of the primary credit reporting bureaus.

Transfer of Ownership Any process in which a property changes hands from one owner to another.

Transfer Tax An amount specified by state or local authorities when ownership in a piece of property changes hands.

Treasury Index A measurement that is used to derive interest rate changes for ARMs.

Triple Net Lease A lease that requires the tenant to pay all property expenses on top of the rental payments.

Trustee A fiduciary who oversees property or funds on behalf of another party.

Truth-in-Lending The federal legislation requiring lenders to fully disclose the terms and conditions of a mortgage in writing.

Turn Key Project A project in which someone other than the owner is responsible for the construction of a building or for tenant improvements.

Two- to Four-Family Property A structure that provides living space for two to four families while ownership is held in a single deed.

Two-Step Mortgage An ARM with two different interest rates: one for the loan's first five or

seven years and another for the remainder of the loan term.

Under Construction The time period that exists after a building's construction has started but before a certificate of occupancy has been presented.

Under Contract The period of time during which a buyer's offer to purchase a property has been accepted, and the buyer is able to finalize financing arrangements without the concern of the seller making a deal with another buyer.

Underwriter A company, usually an investment banking firm, that is involved in a guarantee that an entire issue of stocks or bonds will be purchased.

Underwriters' Knot An approved knot according to code that may be tied at the end of an electrical cord to prevent the wires from being pulled away from their connection to each other or to electrical terminals.

Underwriting The process during which lenders analyze

the risks a particular borrower presents and set appropriate conditions for the loan.

Underwriting Fee A fee that mortgage lenders charge for verifying the information on the loan application and making a final decision on approving the loan.

Unencumbered A term that refers to property free of liens or other encumbrances.

Unimproved Land See: Raw Land.

Unrated Classes Usually the lowest classes securities.

Unrecorded Deed A deed that transfers right of ownership from one owner to another without being officially documented.

Umbrella Partnership Real Estate Investment Trust (UPREIT) An organizational structure in which a REIT's assets are owned by a holding company for tax reasons.

Usable Square Footage The total area that is included within the exterior walls of the tenant's space.

Use The particular purpose for which a property is intended to be employed.

VA Loan A mortgage through the VA program in which a down payment is not necessarily required.

Vacancy Factor The percentage of gross revenue that pro forma income statements expect to be lost due to vacancies.

Vacancy Rate The percentage of space that is available to rent.

Vacant Space Existing rental space that is presently being marketed for lease minus space that is available for sublease.

Value-Added A phrase advisors and managers generally use to describe investments in underperforming and/or undermanaged assets.

Variable Rate Mortgage (VRM) A loan in which the interest rate changes according to fluctuations in particular indexes.

Variable-Rate Also called adjustable-rate. The interest rate on a loan that varies over the term of the loan according to a predetermined index.

Variance A permission that enables a property owner to work around a zoning ordinance's literal requirements which cause a unique hardship due to special circumstances.

Verification of Deposit (VOD) The confirmation statement a borrower's bank may be asked to sign in order to verify the borrower's account balances and history.

Verification of Employment (VOE) The confirmation statement a borrower's employer may be asked to sign in order to verify the borrower's position and salary.

Vested Having the right to draw on a portion or on all of a pension or other retirement fund.

Veterans Administration (VA) A federal government agency that assists veterans in purchasing a home without a down payment.

Virtual Storefront A retail business presence on the Internet.

Waiting Period The period of time between initially filing a registration statement and the date it becomes effective.

Warehouse Fee A closing cost fee that represents the lender's expense of temporarily holding a borrower's loan before it is sold on the secondary mortgage market.

Weighted-Average Coupon The average, using the balance of each mortgage as the weighting factor, of the gross interest rates of the mortgages underlying a pool as of the date of issue.

Weighted-Average Equity The part of the equation that is used to calculate investment-level income, appreciation, and total returns on a quarter-by-quarter basis.

Weighted-Average Rental Rates The average ratio of unequal rental rates across two or more buildings in a market.

Working Drawings The detailed blueprints for a construction project that comprise the contractual documents which describe the exact manner in which a project is to be built.

Workout The strategy in which a borrower negotiates with a lender to attempt to restructure the borrower's debt rather than go through the foreclosure proceedings.

Wraparound Mortgage A loan obtained by a buyer to use for the remaining balance on the seller's first mortgage, as well as an additional amount requested by the seller.

Write-Down A procedure used in accounting when an asset's book value is adjusted downward to reflect current market value more accurately.

Write-Off A procedure used in accounting when an asset is determined to be uncollectible and is therefore considered to be a loss.

Yield Maintenance Premium A penalty the borrower must pay in order to make investors whole in the event of early repayment of principal.

Yield Spread The difference in income derived from a commercial mortgage and from a benchmark value.

Yield The actual return on an investment, usually paid in dividends or interest.

Zoning Ordinance The regulations and laws that control the use or improvement of land in a particular area or zone.

Zoning The act of dividing a city or town into particular areas and applying laws and regulations regarding the architectural design, structure, and intended uses of buildings within those areas.